Collins
First
Dictionary

HarperCollins Publishers
Westerhill Road
Bishopbriggs
Glasgow
G64 2QT

First edition 2014

Impression 10 9 8 7 6 5 4

© HarperCollins Publishers 2014

ISBN 978-0-00-757872-6

Collins® is a registered trademark of
HarperCollins Publishers Limited

www.collinsdictionary.com
www.collins.co.uk

A catalogue record for this book is available
from the British Library

Artwork and design by Q2A Media

Printed and bound in China by
RR Donnelley APS

Images used under licence from
Shutterstock.com

Editors:
Sandra Anderson
Kerry Ferguson
Lorna Gilmour
Patrick Goldsmith
Mike Munro
Elspeth Summers

For the Publisher:
Gerry Breslin
Kerry Ferguson

MIX
Paper from
responsible sources
FSC™ C007454

FSC www.fsc.org

FSC™ is a non-profit international organisation established to promote the
responsible management of the world's forests. Products carrying the FSC
label are independently certified to assure consumers that they come from
forests that are managed to meet the social, economic and ecological needs
of present and future generations, and other controlled sources.

Find out more about HarperCollins and the environment at
www.harpercollins.co.uk/green

How to find a word in this dictionary

It is easy to use a dictionary if you know the alphabetical order of letters.

ate - axe

A B C D E F G H I J K L M N

ate
➡ Look at **eat**.
*He **ate** three apples.*

atlas *noun*
atlases
An **atlas** is a book of maps.

attack *verb*
attacks, attacking, attacked
If someone **attacks** another person, they try to hurt them.

attention *noun*
If you pay **attention**, you watch and listen.
*He always pays **attention** in class.*

attract *verb*
attracts, attracting, attracted
If something **attracts** things to it, it makes them move towards it.
*Magnets **attract** anything made of iron.*

D E F G H I

match *noun*
matches
1 A **match** is a small, thin stick that makes a flame when you rub it on a rough surface.
*She lit a **match** and held it up to the candle.*
2 A **match** is a game of football, cricket, or some other sport.
*We won all our **matches** last year.*

kind *noun*
kinds
A **kind** of thing is a type or sort of that thing.
*What **kind** of car is that?*

kind *adjective*
kinder, kindest
Someone who is **kind** is friendly and helps you.
*Thank you for being so **kind** to me.*

d e f g h i j

1. Think of the first letter, and look at the side of the page to find the right pages in the dictionary.

2. Think of the second letter, and look at the words at the top of the page, to help you find the page you need.

3. Now look down the list of words on the page, to find the word you are looking for.

4. You can check how to spell words.

5. You can see how the word changes when it is used in different ways.

6. You can see what the word means.

7. You can see how the word is used in a sentence.

8. You can see if a word has more than one meaning.

9. You can see if a word is a noun, verb or adjective. Some words can be used in more than one way.

How words work

Nouns

A **noun** is a word that is used for talking about a person or thing.

> **arm** *noun*
> **bird** *noun*
> **car** *noun*

If you have more than one of the thing, you use the word that ends in **-S**.

> **arms**

Some words have special endings, or different spellings, when there is more than one.

> **child → children**

Adjectives

An **adjective** is a word like "big" or "beautiful" that tells you more about a person or thing.

> **happy** *adjective*
> **wild** *adjective*
> **wet** *adjective*

Adjectives can be used in different ways.

> **happier, happiest**
> **wilder, wildest**
> **wetter, wettest**

Verbs

A **verb** is a word like "sing", "feel" or "eat" that you use for saying what someone or something does.

> **eat** *verb*
> **cry** *verb*
> **talk** *verb*

Verbs can be used in different ways.

> **eats, eating, ate, eaten**
> **cries, crying, cried**
> **talks, talking, talked**

Verbs can be used to talk about things that you are doing now.

> *He **teaches** people how to play the piano.*
> *He **is** in the school football team.*

They can be used to talk about things that you did in the past.

> *She **took** the plates into the kitchen.*
> *She **talked** to him on the phone.*

They can also be used to talk about things that you will do in the future.

> *Mum **will** be angry.*
> *Our teacher **will** give the prizes to the winners.*
> ***We'll** come along later.*

Tips to help you become a super speller!

When you have found a word you need in the dictionary, try to learn how to spell it using the "Look, Say, Cover, Write, Check" strategy:

Look at the word carefully.
> Look at its shape and length.
> Look at the letters in it to see if there are any letter patterns that might help you remember how to spell it in future, for example, **bright**, **light**, **tight**.

Say the word out loud.
> Think about how the word sounds! Can you spell a word that sounds like it? Does your word have a similar sound pattern in it? Sound out the word and try to spell it.

Cover the word up so you cannot see it.

Write the word down without looking at it in the dictionary. As you do this, think about how the word looks! Does it look right? Is it the right shape? Is it the right length?

Check that you have written it correctly.

Aa

abacus *noun*
abacuses

An **abacus** is a frame with beads that move along pieces of wire. It is used for counting.

able *adjective*

If you are **able** to do something, you know how to do it.
*She is **able** to swim.*

about

1 **About** means to do with.
   *This book is **about** history.*

2 **About** also means near to something.
   *His grandfather is **about** 80 years old.*

above

If something is **above** another thing, it is over it or higher than it.
*Lift the ball **above** your head.*

accident *noun*
accidents

1 An **accident** is something nasty that happens, and that hurts someone.
   *He broke his leg in a car **accident**.*

2 If something happens by **accident**, you do not expect it to happen.
   *I dropped a cup by **accident**.*

ache *verb*
aches, aching, ached

If a part of your body **aches**, you feel a steady pain there.
*My leg **aches** a lot.*

acorn *noun*
acorns

An **acorn** is the seed of an oak tree.

across

If someone goes **across** a place, they go from one side of it to the other.
*She walked **across** the road.*

act *verb*
acts, acting, acted

1 When you **act**, you do something.
   *The police **acted** quickly to stop the fight.*

2 If you **act** in a play or film, you pretend to be one of the people in it.

active *adjective*

Someone who is **active** moves around a lot.
*My grandmother is very **active** for her age.*

add *verb*
adds, adding, added

1 If you **add** one thing to another, you put it with the other thing.
   ***Add** the water to the flour.*

2 If you **add** numbers together, you find out how many they make together.
   ***Add** three and six.*

address *noun*
addresses

Your **address** is the name of the place where you live.

adjective *noun*
adjectives

An **adjective** is a word like "big" or "beautiful", that tells you more about a person or thing.

A
B
C
D
E
F
G
H
I
J
K
L
M
N
O
P
Q
R
S
T
U
V
W
X
Y
Z

admire *verb*
admires, admiring, admired

If you **admire** something, you like it and think that it is very nice or very good.
*I **admired** his painting.*

adopt *verb*
adopts, adopting, adopted

If you **adopt** another person's child, you take them into your own family as your son or daughter.

adult *noun*
adults

An **adult** is a person who is not a child anymore.

adventure *noun*
adventures

An **adventure** is something exciting which you do, or which happens to you.
*He wrote a book about his **adventures** in the jungle.*

adverb *noun*
adverbs

An **adverb** is a word like "slowly", "now", or "very" that tells you about how something is done.

aeroplane *noun*
aeroplanes

An **aeroplane** is a large vehicle with wings and engines that flies through the air.

afraid *adjective*

If you are **afraid**, you are frightened because you think that something bad will happen to you.
*I am not **afraid** of the dark.*

after

1 If something happens **after** another thing, it happens later than it.
*I watched television **after** dinner.*

2 If you go **after** a person or thing, you follow them or chase them.
*They ran **after** her.*

afternoon *noun*
afternoons

The **afternoon** is the part of each day between twelve noon and about six o'clock.

again

If something happens **again**, it happens another time.
*We went to the park **again** yesterday.*

against

1 If something is **against** another thing, it is touching it.
*He leaned **against** the wall.*

2 If you play **against** someone in a game, you try to beat them.
*The two teams played **against** one another.*

age *noun*
ages

Your **age** is the number of years that you have lived.

ago

You use **ago** to talk about a time in the past.
*She left two weeks **ago**.*

agree *verb*
agrees, agreeing, agreed

If you **agree** with someone, you think the same as they do about something.
*I **agree** with you about him.*

ahead

Someone who is **ahead** of another person is in front of them.
*My brother ran **ahead** of us.*

air *noun*

Air is the mixture of gases all around us that we breathe.
*I opened the window and let in some **air**.*

aircraft *noun*
aircraft

An **aircraft** is any vehicle which can fly.

airport *noun*
airports

An **airport** is a place where aeroplanes fly from and land.

alarm *noun*
alarms

An **alarm** is a piece of equipment that warns you of danger by making a noise.
*The car **alarm** woke us up.*

alien *noun*
aliens

In stories and films, an **alien** is a creature from another planet.

alike *adjective*

If people or things are **alike**, they are the same in some way.
*The two cats looked **alike**.*

alive *adjective*

If a person, an animal or a plant is **alive**, they are living and not dead.

all

You use **all** to talk about everything, everyone, or the whole of something.
*Did you eat **all** of it?*

alligator *noun*
alligators

An **alligator** is a large reptile with a long body, a long mouth and sharp teeth. **Alligators'** mouths are in the shape of a letter U.

allow *verb*
allows, allowing, allowed

If you **allow** someone to do something, you let them do it.
*Mum **allowed** us to go out and play.*

a
b
c
d
e
f
g
h
i
j
k
l
m
n
o
p
q
r
s
t
u
v
w
x
y
z

A
B
C
D
E
F
G
H
I
J
K
L
M
N
O
P
Q
R
S
T
U
V
W
X
Y
Z

all right or alright *adjective*

If you say that something is **all right**, you mean that it is good enough.
*I thought the film was **all right**.*

almost

Almost means very nearly.
*I **almost** missed the bus.*

alone *adjective*

When you are **alone**, you are not with any other people.
*She was **alone** in the room.*

along

1 If you walk **along** a road or other place, you move towards one end of it.
*We walked **along** the street.*

2 If you bring something **along** when you go somewhere, you bring it with you.
*She brought a present **along** to the party.*

aloud

When you read or talk **aloud**, you read or talk so that other people can hear you.
*She read the story **aloud** to us.*

alphabet *noun*
alphabets

An **alphabet** is a set of letters that is used for writing words. The letters are arranged in a special order.
*A is the first letter of the **alphabet**.*

already

You use **already** to show that something has happened before the present time.
*She is **already** here.*

also

You use **also** to give more information about something.
*I'm cold, and I'm **also** hungry.*

always

If you **always** do something, you do it every time or all the time.
*She's **always** late for school.*

am

⇨ Look at **be**.
*I **am** six years old.*

amazing *adjective*

You say that something is **amazing** when it is a surprise and you like it.
*We had an **amazing** holiday.*

ambulance *noun*
ambulances

An **ambulance** is a vehicle for taking people to hospital.

amount *noun*
amounts

An **amount** of something is how much there is of it.
*We only have a small **amount** of food.*

amphibian *noun*
amphibians

frog

An **amphibian** is an animal that lives both on land and in water, for example a frog or a toad.

ancient *adjective*

Ancient means very old, or from a long time ago.
They lived in an ***ancient*** *castle.*

angry *adjective*
angrier, angriest

When you are **angry**, you feel very upset about something.
She was ***angry*** *at her brother for breaking the window.*

animal *noun*
animals

An **animal** is any creature that is alive, but not a plant or a person.

ankle *noun*
ankles

Your **ankle** is the part of your body where your foot joins your leg.
I fell and twisted my ***ankle****.*

annoy *verb*
annoys, annoying, annoyed

If something **annoys** you, it makes you angry and upset.
It ***annoys*** *me when people are rude.*

another

You use **another** to mean one more.
She ate ***another*** *cake.*

answer *verb*
answers, answering, answered

If you **answer** someone, you say something back to them.
She said hello, but he didn't ***answer****.*

ant *noun*
ants

Ants are small insects that live in large groups.

antelope *noun*
antelopes

An **antelope** is an animal that looks like a deer.

any

1   You use **any** to mean some of a thing.
    Is there ***any*** *juice left?*

2   You also use **any** to show that it does not matter which one.
    Take ***any*** *book you want.*

anybody

You use **anybody** to talk about a person, when it does not matter which one.
Is there ***anybody*** *there?*

anyone

You use **anyone** to talk about a person, when it does not matter who.
Don't tell ***anyone****.*

anything

You use **anything** to talk about a thing, when it does not matter which one.
I can't see ***anything****.*

a
b
c
d
e
f
g
h
i
j
k
l
m
n
o
p
q
r
s
t
u
v
w
x
y
z

A
B
C
D
E
F
G
H
I
J
K
L
M
N
O
P
Q
R
S
T
U
V
W
X
Y
Z

anywhere

You use **anywhere** to talk about a place, when it does not matter which one.
*You can go **anywhere** you like.*

apart

1 When things are **apart**, there is a space or a distance between them.
   *The desks are too far **apart**.*

2 If you take something **apart**, you take it to pieces.
   *He took his bike **apart**.*

ape *noun*
apes

An **ape** is an animal like a large monkey with long, strong arms and no tail.

apologize
or **apologise** *verb*

apologizes, apologizing, apologized

When you **apologize**, you say that you are sorry for something you have said or done.
*He **apologized** for breaking the window.*

appear *verb*
appears, appearing, appeared

When something **appears**, it becomes possible to see it.
*The sun **appeared** from behind the clouds.*

apple *noun*
apples

An **apple** is a firm, round fruit with green, red, or yellow skin.

April *noun*

April is the month after March and before May. It has 30 days.
*His birthday is in **April**.*

apron *noun*
aprons

An **apron** is a large piece of cloth that you wear over your other clothes to keep them clean when you are cooking or painting.

are
⇨ Look at **be**.
*They **are** both in my class.*

area *noun*
areas

An **area** is a part of a place.
*We live in an **area** near the park.*

aren't

Aren't is short for **are not**.
*My friends **aren't** here today.*

argue *verb*
argues, arguing, argued

If you **argue** with someone, you talk about something that you do not agree about.
*We **argued** about where to go.*

argument *noun*
arguments

If you have an **argument** with someone, you talk about something that you do not agree about.
*She had an **argument** with another girl.*

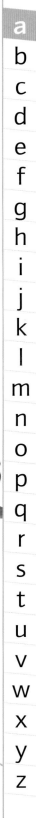

arm *noun*
arms

arm

Your **arms** are the two parts of your body between your shoulders and your hands.
*She stretched her **arms** out.*

armchair *noun*
armchairs

An **armchair** is a big comfortable chair with parts on the sides for you to put your arms on.

army *noun*
armies

An **army** is a large group of soldiers who fight in a war.

around

1 **Around** means in a circle.
   *There were lots of people **around** her.*

2 You also use **around** to say that something is in every part of a place.
   *His toys lay **around** the room.*

3 **Around** also means near to something.
   *We left **around** noon.*

arrange *verb*
arranges, arranging, arranged

1 If you **arrange** something, you make plans for it to happen.
   *We **arranged** a party for her birthday.*

2 If you **arrange** things somewhere, you put them in a way that looks tidy or pretty.
   *He **arranged** the books in piles.*

arrive *verb*
arrives, arriving, arrived

When you **arrive** at a place, you get there.
*We **arrived** ten minutes late.*

arrow *noun*
arrows

1 An **arrow** is a long, thin stick with a sharp point at one end.
   *The soldiers used bows and **arrows**.*

2 An **arrow** is also a sign that shows you which way to go.
   *Follow the **arrows** along the path.*

art *noun*

Art is something that someone has made for people to look at, for example a painting or drawing.

ask *verb*
asks, asking, asked

1 If you **ask** someone a question, you say that you want to know something.
   *I **asked** him what his name was.*

2 If you **ask** for something, you say that you want it.
   *She **asked** for some sweets.*

asleep *adjective*

If you are **asleep**, you are sleeping.
*The cat was **asleep** under the tree.*

assembly *noun*
assemblies

An **assembly** is a group of people who meet together.
*We were late for school **assembly**.*

assistant *noun*
assistants

An **assistant** is someone who helps another person in their work.

astronaut *noun*
astronauts

An **astronaut** is a person who travels in space.

a b c d e f g h i j k l m n o p q r s t u v w x y z

7

B
C
D
E
F
G
H
I
J
K
L
M
N
O
P
Q
R
S
T
U
V
W
X
Y
Z

ate

⇨ Look at **eat**.

*He **ate** three apples.*

atlas *noun*
atlases

An **atlas** is a book of maps.

attack *verb*
attacks, attacking, attacked

If someone **attacks** another person, they try to hurt them.

attention *noun*

If you pay **attention**, you watch and listen.
*He always pays **attention** in class.*

attract *verb*
attracts, attracting, attracted

If something **attracts** things to it, it makes them move towards it.
*Magnets **attract** anything made of iron.*

audience *noun*
audiences

An **audience** is all of the people who watch or listen to something, for example a film or a play.

August *noun*

August is the month after July and before September. It has 31 days.
*We went on holiday in **August**.*

aunt *noun*
aunts

Your **aunt** is the sister of your mother or father, or the wife of your uncle.

author *noun*
authors

An **author** is a person who writes books.

autumn *noun*
autumns

Autumn is the season after summer and before winter. In the **autumn** the weather usually becomes cooler and the leaves fall off the trees.

awake *adjective*

Someone who is **awake** is not sleeping.
*I stayed **awake** until midnight.*

away

1 If someone moves **away** from a place, they move so that they are not there any more.
*He walked **away** from the house.*

2 If you put something **away**, you put it where it should be.
*Put your books **away** before you go.*

awful *adjective*

If something is **awful**, it is very bad.
*There was an **awful** smell.*

axe *noun*
axes

An **axe** is a tool with a handle and a big, sharp blade. It is used to chop wood.

Bb

baby *noun*
babies

A **baby** is a very young child.

back *noun*
backs

1 Your **back** is the part of your body from your neck to your bottom.
*He was lying on his **back** in the grass.*

2 The **back** of something is the side or part of it that is farthest from the front.
*She was in a room at the **back** of the shop.*

backwards

1 If you move **backwards**, you move in the direction behind you.
*She walked **backwards**.*

2 If you do something **backwards**, you do it the opposite of the usual way.
*He had his jumper on **backwards**.*

bad *adjective*
worse, worst

1 Something that is **bad** is not nice or good.
*The weather is **bad** today.*

2 Someone who is **bad** does things they should not do.
*Some **bad** boys stole the money.*

badge *noun*
badges

A **badge** is a small piece of metal or plastic with words or a picture on it that you wear on your clothes.

badger *noun*
badgers

A **badger** is an animal that has a white head with two black stripes on it. **Badgers** live beneath the ground and come out at night.

bag *noun*
bags

A **bag** is a container that you use to hold or carry things.
*He put his shoes in his **bag**.*

bake *verb*
bakes, baking, baked

When you **bake** food, you cook it in an oven.

baker *noun*
bakers

A **baker** is a person who makes and sells bread and cakes.

balance *verb*
balances, balancing, balanced

When you **balance** something, you keep it steady and do not let it fall.
*She **balanced** a book on her head.*

ball *noun*
balls

A **ball** is a round thing that you kick, throw or catch in games.

ballet *noun*

Ballet is a kind of dance with special steps that often tells a story.

a
b
c
d
e
f
g
h
i
j
k
l
m
n
o
p
q
r
s
t
u
v
w
x
y
z

9

A
B
C
D
E
F
G
H
I
J
K
L
M
N
O
P
Q
R
S
T
U
V
W
X
Y
Z

balloon *noun*
balloons

A **balloon** is a small bag made of thin rubber that you blow into to make it bigger.

banana *noun*
bananas

A **banana** is a long curved fruit with a thick yellow skin.

band *noun*
bands

1 A **band** is a group of people who play music together.
   *He plays the guitar in a **band**.*

2 A **band** is also a narrow strip of material that you put around something.
   *She wore a **band** round her hair.*

bandage *noun*
bandages

A **bandage** is a long strip of cloth that you wrap around a part of your body when you have hurt it.

bang *noun*
bangs

A **bang** is a sudden, loud noise.
*The balloon burst with a **bang**.*

bank *noun*
banks

1 A **bank** is a place where people can keep their money.
   *He got some money from the **bank**.*

2 A **bank** is also the ground beside a river.
   *We walked along the **bank**.*

bar *noun*
bars

A **bar** is a long, thin piece of wood or metal.
*There were **bars** on the windows.*

bare *adjective*
barer, barest

1 If a part of your body is **bare**, it is not covered by any clothes.
   *Her feet were **bare**.*

2 If something is **bare**, it has nothing on top of it or inside it.
   *The cupboard was **bare**.*

bark *verb*
barks, barking, barked

When a dog **barks**, it makes a short, loud noise.

barn *noun*
barns

A **barn** is a big building on a farm where animals and crops are kept.

base *noun*
bases

The **base** of something is the lowest part of it, or the part that it stands on.
*She stood at the **base** of the stairs.*

basket *noun*
baskets

A **basket** is a container that you use to hold or carry things. It is made from thin strips of material.

bat *noun*
bats

1 A **bat** is a special stick that you use to hit a ball in some games.

2 A **bat** is also a small animal that looks like a mouse with wings. **Bats** come out to fly at night.

bath *noun*
baths

A **bath** is a long container that you fill with water and sit in to wash yourself.

bathroom *noun*
bathrooms

A **bathroom** is a room with a bath or shower in it.

battery *noun*
batteries

A **battery** is a small tube or box for storing electricity. You put **batteries** in things like toys and radios to make them work.
*The clock needs a new **battery**.*

be *verb*
am, is, are, being, was, were, been

1 You use **be** to say what a person or thing is like.
*She **is** very young.*

2 You also use **be** to say that something is there.
*There **is** a tree in the garden.*

beach *noun*
beaches

A **beach** is the land by the edge of the sea. It is covered with sand or stones.

bead *noun*
beads

A **bead** is a small piece of glass, wood or plastic with a hole through the middle. You put **beads** on a string to make necklaces or bracelets.

beak *noun*
beaks

A bird's **beak** is the hard part of its mouth.

bean *noun*
beans

A **bean** is the small seed of some plants that you can eat as a vegetable.

bear *noun*
bears

A **bear** is a big, strong animal with thick fur and sharp claws.

beard *noun*
beards

A **beard** is the hair that grows on a man's chin and cheeks.

beat *verb*
beats, beating, beat, beaten

1 If you **beat** something, you keep hitting it.
*He **beat** the drum with a stick.*

2 If you **beat** someone in a game or a competition, you do better than they do.
*He **beat** me in the race.*

beautiful
adjective

If something is **beautiful**, it is very nice to look at or to listen to.
*He painted a **beautiful** picture.*

became
⇨ Look at **become**.
*She **became** very angry.*

a
b
c
d
e
f
g
h
i
j
k
l
m
n
o
p
q
r
s
t
u
v
w
x
y
z

A
B
C
D
E
F
G
H
I
J
K
L
M
N
O
P
Q
R
S
T
U
V
W
X
Y
Z

because

You use **because** to say why something happens.
*I went to bed **because** I was tired.*

become *verb*
becomes, becoming, became, become

If one thing **becomes** another thing, it starts to be that thing.
*The weather **became** cold.*

bed *noun*
beds

A **bed** is a piece of furniture that you lie on when you sleep.

bedroom *noun*
bedrooms

A **bedroom** is a room with a bed in it where you sleep.

bedtime *noun*
bedtimes

Your **bedtime** is the time when you usually go to bed.
*My **bedtime** is at eight o'clock.*

bee *noun*
bees

A **bee** is an insect with wings and black and yellow stripes on its body.
Bees live in large groups and make honey.

been
⇨ Look at **be**.
*We have always **been** good friends.*

beetle *noun*
beetles

A **beetle** is an insect with hard wings that cover its body when it is not flying.

before

If one thing happens **before** another thing, it happens earlier than it.
*My birthday is just **before** his.*

began
⇨ Look at **begin**.
*She **began** to laugh.*

begin *verb*
begins, beginning, began, begun

If you **begin** to do something, you start to do it.
*You can **begin** to write now.*

begun
⇨ Look at **begin**.
*He has **begun** to play the piano.*

behave *verb*
behaves, behaving, behaved

1   The way you **behave** is the way that you do and say things.
    *She **behaves** like a baby.*

2   If you **behave** yourself, you are good.
    *You can come if you **behave** yourself.*

behind

If something is **behind** another thing, it is at the back of it.
*He stood **behind** his desk.*

believe *verb*
believes, believing, believed

If you **believe** something, you think that it is true.
I don't believe that story.

bell *noun*
bells

A **bell** is a piece of metal in the shape of a cup that rings when you shake it or hit it.

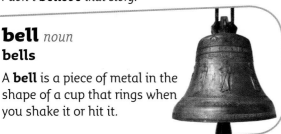

belong *verb*
belongs, belonging, belonged

1 If something **belongs** to you, it is yours.
The book belongs to her.

2 If you **belong** to a group of people, you are one of them.
He belongs to our team.

3 If something **belongs** somewhere, that is where it should be.
Your toys belong in your room.

below

If something is **below** another thing, it is lower down than it.
His shoes were below his bed.

belt *noun*
belts

A **belt** is a band of leather or cloth that you wear around your waist.

bench *noun*
benches

A **bench** is a long seat that two or more people can sit on.

bend *verb*
bends, bending, bent

When you **bend** something, you change its shape so that it is not straight any more.
Bend your legs when you do this exercise.

beneath

If something is **beneath** another thing, it is below it.
The dog was beneath the table.

bent

⇨ Look at **bend**.
He bent to pick up the bags.

berry *noun*
berries

A **berry** is a small, soft fruit that grows on a bush or a tree.

beside

If something is **beside** another thing, it is next to it.
He sat down beside me.

best

If you say that something is **best**, you mean that it is better than all the others.
You are my best friend.

a
b
c
d
e
f
g
h
i
j
k
l
m
n
o
p
q
r
s
t
u
v
w
x
y
z

A
B
C
D
E
F
G
H
I
J
K
L
M
N
O
P
Q
R
S
T
U
V
W
X
Y
Z

better

1   You use **better** to mean that a thing is very good compared to another thing.
*His painting is **better** than mine.*

2   If you feel **better**, you do not feel ill any more.
*I feel much **better** today.*

between

If you are **between** two things, one of them is on one side of you and the other is on the other side.
*She stood **between** her two brothers.*

bicycle *noun*
bicycles

A **bicycle** is a vehicle with two wheels. You push the pedals with your feet to make the wheels turn.

big *adjective*
bigger, biggest

A person or thing that is **big** is large in size.
*She lives in a **big** house.*

bike *noun*
bikes

A **bike** is a bicycle or motorbike.

bin *noun*
bins

A **bin** is a container that you put rubbish in.

bird *noun*
birds

A **bird** is an animal with feathers, wings, and a beak. Most **birds** can fly.

birthday *noun*
birthdays

Your **birthday** is the date that you were born.
*She gave me a present on my **birthday**.*

biscuit *noun*
biscuits

A **biscuit** is a kind of small, hard, dry cake.

bit *noun*
bits

A **bit** of something is a small amount of it, or a small part of it.
*I ate a **bit** of bread.*

bite *verb*
bites, biting, bit, bitten

If you **bite** something, you use your teeth to cut into it.
*The dog tried to **bite** him.*

black *noun/adjective*

Black is the colour of the sky at night.
*The car is **black**.*

blackboard *noun*
blackboards

A **blackboard** is a flat, black surface that you write on with chalk in a classroom.

blade *noun*
blades

A **blade** is the flat, sharp part of a knife that you use to cut things.

blame *verb*
blames, blaming, blamed

If you **blame** someone for something bad, you think that they made it happen.
*Mum **blamed** me for making the mess.*

blanket *noun*
blankets

A **blanket** is a large, thick piece of cloth that you put on a bed to keep you warm.

blew

➩ Look at **blow**.
*The wind **blew** outside.*

blind *adjective*

Someone who is **blind** cannot see.

block *noun*
blocks

A **block** of something is a large piece of it with straight sides.
*We made a house with **blocks** of wood.*

blood *noun*

Blood is the red liquid that moves around inside your body.

blouse *noun*
blouses

A **blouse** is something a girl or woman can wear. It covers the top part of the body and has buttons down the front.

blow *verb*
blows, blowing, blew, blown

1 When the wind **blows**, it moves the air.
2 When you **blow**, you push air out of your mouth.
   *He **blew** on his hands to keep them warm.*

blue *noun/adjective*

Blue is the colour of the sky on a sunny day.
*Her dress is **blue**.*

blunt *adjective*
blunter, bluntest

Something that is **blunt** does not have a sharp point or edge.
*My pencil is **blunt**.*

boat *noun*
boats

A **boat** is a small vehicle that carries people on water.

body *noun*
bodies

A person's or animal's **body** is all their parts.
*It's fun to stretch and twist your **body**.*

boil *verb*
boils, boiling, boiled

1 When water **boils**, it becomes very hot, and you can see bubbles in it and steam coming from it.
2 When you **boil** food, you cook it in water that is boiling.

bone *noun*
bones

Your **bones** are the hard parts inside your body.
*I broke a **bone** in my leg.*

a
b
c
d
e
f
g
h
i
j
k
l
m
n
o
p
q
r
s
t
u
v
w
x
y
z

A
B
C
D
E
F
G
H
I
J
K
L
M
N
O
P
Q
R
S
T
U
V
W
X
Y
Z

bonfire *noun*
bonfires

A **bonfire** is a big fire that is made outside.

book *noun*
books

A **book** is a set of pages with words or pictures on them, that are held together inside a cover.

boot *noun*
boots

A **boot** is a kind of shoe that covers your foot and the lower part of your leg.

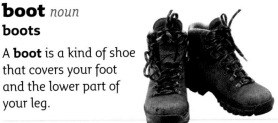

bored *adjective*

If you are **bored**, you feel annoyed because you have nothing to do.

boring *adjective*

If something is **boring**, it is not interesting.

born *verb*

When a baby is **born**, it comes out of its mother's body.
*My sister was **born** three years ago.*

borrow *verb*
borrows, borrowing, borrowed

If you **borrow** something from someone, they let you have it for a short time and then you give it back.
*Can I **borrow** your pen, please?*

both

You use **both** to mean two people or two things together.
*He put **both** books into the drawer.*

bottle *noun*
bottles

A **bottle** is a container made of glass or plastic that holds liquid.

bottom *noun*
bottoms

1 The **bottom** of something is its lowest part.
2 Your **bottom** is the part of your body that you sit on.

bought
⇨ Look at **buy**.
*We **bought** bread and milk.*

bounce *verb*
bounces, bouncing, bounced

When something **bounces**, it hits another thing and then moves away from it again.
*The ball **bounced** across the floor.*

bow *verb*
bows, bowing, bowed

When you **bow**, you bend your body towards someone as a polite way of saying hello or thanking them.
*They all **bowed** to the king.*

bow *noun*
bows

1 A **bow** is a knot with two loose ends that you use to tie laces and ribbons.
2 A **bow** is also a long, curved piece of wood with a string stretched between the two ends, that is used to send arrows through the air.

16

bowl *noun*
bowls

A **bowl** is a round container that you use to hold food or drink.

box *noun*
boxes

A **box** is a container with a hard, straight bottom and sides, and usually a lid.

boy *noun*
boys

A **boy** is a male child.

bracelet *noun*
bracelets

A **bracelet** is a chain or a band that you wear around your wrist.

brain *noun*
brains

Your **brain** is inside your head. It controls your body and lets you think and feel things.

branch *noun*
branches

The **branches** of a tree are the parts that grow out from its trunk and have leaves on them.

brave *adjective*
braver, bravest

If you are **brave**, you are not afraid of something dangerous.

bread *noun*

Bread is a food that is made from flour and water and baked in an oven.

break *verb*
breaks, breaking, broke, broken

1 When something **breaks**, it goes into pieces.
 *I dropped a plate and it **broke**.*

2 When a machine **breaks**, it stops working.
 *My brother **broke** the television.*

breakfast *noun*
breakfasts

Breakfast is the first meal of the day.

breathe *verb*
breathes, breathing, breathed

When you **breathe**, air goes in and out of your body through your nose or your mouth.

brick *noun*
bricks

Bricks are small blocks of baked earth used for building.

bride *noun*
brides

A **bride** is a woman who is getting married.

a
b
c
d
e
f
g
h
i
j
k
l
m
n
o
p
q
r
s
t
u
v
w
x
y
z

A
B
C
D
E
F
G
H
I
J
K
L
M
N
O
P
Q
R
S
T
U
V
W
X
Y
Z

bridegroom *noun*
bridegrooms

A **bridegroom** is a man who is getting married.

bridge *noun*
bridges

A **bridge** is something that is built over a river, a road, or a railway so that people can get across it.

bright *adjective*
brighter, brightest

1 A **bright** colour is very easy to see.
   *She wore a **bright** red dress.*

2 Something that is **bright** shines with a lot of light.
   *The sun is very **bright** today.*

brilliant *adjective*

Something that is **brilliant** is very good.
*I thought the film was **brilliant**.*

bring *verb*
brings, bringing, brought

If you **bring** something, you take it with you when you go somewhere.
*You can **bring** a friend to the party.*

broke
⇨ Look at **break**.
*I'm sorry I **broke** the radio.*

broken *adjective*

If something is **broken**, it is in pieces.
*All of his toys are **broken**.*

broom *noun*
brooms

A **broom** is a brush with a long handle that you use to sweep the floor.

brother *noun*
brothers

Your **brother** is a boy or a man who has the same mother and father as you do.

brought
⇨ Look at **bring**.
*We **brought** some food for the picnic.*

brown *noun/adjective*

Brown is the colour of earth or wood.
*Her eyes are dark **brown**.*

bruise *noun*
bruises

A **bruise** is a purple mark on your skin that appears if something hits a part of your body.
*She has a big **bruise** on her leg.*

brush *noun*
brushes

A **brush** has lots of short hairs fixed to a handle. You use a **brush** to make your hair tidy, to clean things, or to paint.

bubble *noun*
bubbles

A **bubble** is a small ball of liquid with air inside it.

bucket *noun*
buckets

A **bucket** is a deep, round container with a handle that you use to hold or carry liquids.

buckle *noun*
buckles

A **buckle** is something you use to fasten a belt, a shoe or a bag.

bud *noun*
buds

A **bud** is a small, new part on a tree or plant that grows into a leaf or a flower.

build *verb*
builds, building, built

If you **build** something, you make it by putting the parts of it together.
*They are going to **build** the school here.*

building *noun*
buildings

A **building** is a place with walls and a roof.

*Houses, shops and schools are all **buildings**.*

built
⇨ Look at **build**.
*We **built** our house on a hill.*

bulb *noun*
bulbs

A **bulb** is the part of a lamp that is made of glass and gives out light.

bull *noun*
bulls

A **bull** is a male cow. **Bulls** have horns.

bump *verb*
bumps, bumping, bumped

If you **bump** something, or **bump** into it, you hit it without meaning to.
*I **bumped** the table with my bag.*

bunch *noun*
bunches

A **bunch** of things is a group of them.
*He held a **bunch** of keys.*

bundle *noun*
bundles

A **bundle** is a lot of clothes, sticks or other things that are fastened together.

buried
⇨ Look at **bury**.
*The pirates **buried** the gold beneath a tree.*

burn *verb*
burns, burning, burned, burnt

1 If you **burn** something, you destroy it or damage it with fire.
   *He **burned** all the rubbish.*

2 If you **burn** yourself, you touch something that is hot and get hurt.
   *I **burned** myself on the hot iron.*

3 If something is **burning**, it is on fire.
   *The bonfire is still **burning**.*

a
b
c
d
e
f
g
h
i
j
k
l
m
n
o
p
q
r
s
t
u
v
w
x
y
z

A
B
C
D
E
F
G
H
I
J
K
L
M
N
O
P
Q
R
S
T
U
V
W
X
Y
Z

burst *verb*
**bursts,
bursting, burst**

When something **bursts**, it breaks open suddenly.
*The bag **burst** and everything fell out of it.*

bury *verb*
buries, burying, buried

If you **bury** something, you put it into a hole in the ground and cover it up.
*Squirrels **bury** nuts to eat in the winter.*

bus *noun*
buses

A **bus** is a large vehicle that carries lots of people.
*I go to school on the **bus**.*

bush *noun*
bushes

A **bush** is a plant with lots of leaves and branches that is smaller than a tree.

busy *adjective*
busier, busiest

1 If you are **busy**, you have a lot of things to do.
    *We were **busy** cleaning the house.*

2 A **busy** place is full of people.
    *The shops are **busy** today.*

butcher *noun*
butchers

A **butcher** is a person who sells meat.

butter *noun*

Butter is a soft yellow and white food that is made from cream. You spread it on bread or cook with it.

butterfly *noun*
butterflies

A **butterfly** is an insect with four large wings.

button *noun*
buttons

Buttons are small, round things on clothes that you push through holes to fasten the clothes together.

buy *verb*
buys, buying, bought

If you **buy** something, you pay money so that you can have it.
*We went into the shop to **buy** sweets.*

buzz *verb*
buzzes, buzzing, buzzed

If something **buzzes**, it makes a sound like a bee makes when it flies.
*An insect **buzzed** around my head.*

Cc

cabbage *noun*
cabbages

A **cabbage** is a round vegetable with green, white, or purple leaves.

cage *noun*
cages

A **cage** is a box or a room made of bars where you keep birds or animals.

cake *noun*
cakes

A **cake** is a sweet food made from flour, eggs, sugar, and butter that you bake in an oven.

calculator *noun*
calculators

A **calculator** is a small machine that you use to do sums.

calendar *noun*
calendars

A **calendar** is a list of all the days, weeks, and months in a year.

calf *noun*
calves

1 A **calf** is a young cow.
2 Your **calves** are also the thick parts at the backs of your legs, between your ankles and your knees.

call *verb*
calls, calling, called

1 If you **call** someone something, you give them a name.
   *I **called** my cat Pippin.*
2 If you **call** something, you say it in a loud voice.
   *Someone **called** his name.*
3 If you **call** someone, you talk to them on the telephone.
   *I'll **call** you tomorrow.*

calves

⇨ Look at **calf**.
*My **calves** hurt.*

came

⇨ Look at **come**.
*My friends **came** to play at my house.*

camel *noun*
camels

A **camel** is a large animal with one or two big lumps on its back. **Camels** live in hot, dry places and carry people and things.

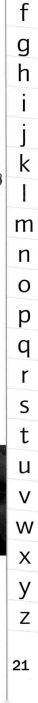

camera *noun*
cameras

A **camera** is a machine that you use to take pictures.

camp *noun*
camps

A **camp** is a place where people live in tents for a short time.

can *verb*
could

If you **can** do something, you are able to do it.
*I **can** swim.*

a
b
c
d
e
f
g
h
i
j
k
l
m
n
o
p
q
r
s
t
u
v
w
x
y
z

A
B
C
D
E
F
G
H
I
J
K
L
M
N
O
P
Q
R
S
T
U
V
W
X
Y
Z

can *noun*
cans

A **can** is a metal container for food or drink.
*She opened a **can** of soup.*

candle *noun*
candles

A **candle** is a stick of wax with a piece of string through the middle that you burn to give you light.

cannot *verb*

If you **cannot** do something, you are not able to do it.
*I **cannot** find my bag.*

can't

Can't is short for **cannot**.
*He **can't** play the piano.*

capital *noun*
capitals

1 The **capital** of a country is the main city, where the country's leaders work.
  *Paris is the **capital** of France.*

2 A **capital** is also a big letter of the alphabet, for example A or R.

car *noun*
cars

A **car** is a vehicle with four wheels and an engine that can carry a small number of people.

card *noun*
cards

1 **Card** is stiff paper.

2 A **card** is a folded piece of stiff paper that has a picture on the front and a message inside. You send **cards** to people at special times, like birthdays.

3 **Cards** are pieces of stiff paper with numbers or pictures on them that you use for playing games.

cardboard *noun*

Cardboard is very thick, stiff paper that is used for making boxes.

care *verb*
cares, caring, cared

1 If you **care** about something, you think that it is important.
  *He doesn't **care** about the way he looks.*

2 If you **care** for a person or an animal, you look after them.
  *She **cared** for her pets.*

careful *adjective*

If you are **careful**, you think about what you are doing so that you do not make any mistakes.
*Be **careful** when you cross the road.*

careless *adjective*

If you are **careless**, you do not think about what you are doing, so that you make mistakes.
*It was **careless** of me to forget my keys.*

carpet *noun*
carpets

A **carpet** is a thick, soft cover for a floor.

carpet

carrot *noun*
carrots

A **carrot** is a long, orange vegetable.

carry *verb*
carries, carrying, carried

If you **carry** something, you hold it and take it somewhere with you.
*We **carried** our bags to the car.*

carton noun
cartons

A **carton** is a container made of plastic or cardboard that is used to hold food or drink.
*I bought a **carton** of milk.*

cartoon noun
cartoons

1 A **cartoon** is a funny drawing.
2 A **cartoon** is also a film that uses drawings, not real people or things.

case noun
cases

A **case** is a container that is used to hold or carry something.
*He put the camera in its **case**.*

castle noun
castles

A **castle** is a large building with very thick, high walls. Most **castles** were built a long time ago to keep the people inside safe from their enemies.

cat noun
cats

A **cat** is an animal that is covered with fur and has a long tail. People often keep small **cats** as pets. Large **cats**, for example lions and tigers, are wild.

catch verb
catches, catching, caught

1 If you **catch** something that is moving, you take hold of it while it is in the air.
   *I tried to **catch** the ball.*
2 If you **catch** a bus or a train, you get on it.
   *We **caught** the bus to school.*
3 If you **catch** an illness, you become ill with it.
   *He **caught** measles.*

caterpillar noun
caterpillars

A **caterpillar** is a small animal that looks like a worm with lots of short legs. **Caterpillars** turn into butterflies or moths.

cattle noun

Cattle are cows and bulls.
*There were **cattle** in the field.*

caught
⇨ Look at **catch**.
*I jumped and **caught** the ball.*

cauliflower noun
cauliflowers

A **cauliflower** is a big, round, white vegetable with green leaves.

cave noun
caves

A **cave** is a big hole in the side of a hill or a mountain, or beneath the ground.

CD noun
CDs

CD is short for compact disc.
*I bought the band's new **CD**.*

a
b
c
d
e
f
g
h
i
j
k
l
m
n
o
p
q
r
s
t
u
v
w
x
y
z

23

A
B
C
D
E
F
G
H
I
J
K
L
M
N
O
P
Q
R
S
T
U
V
W
X
Y
Z

ceiling *noun*
ceilings

A **ceiling** is the part of a room that is above your head.

centimetre *noun*
centimetres

A **centimetre** is used for measuring the length of something. There are ten millimetres in a **centimetre**, and one hundred **centimetres** in a metre.

centre *noun*
centres

The **centre** of something is the middle of it.
*She stood in the **centre** of the room.*

cereal *noun*
cereals

1 A **cereal** is a food made from grains that you eat with milk for breakfast.
2 A **cereal** is also a kind of plant, for example wheat or rice. The seeds of **cereals** are used for food.

chain *noun*
chains

A **chain** is a row of rings made of metal that are joined together in a line.

chair *noun*
chairs

A **chair** is a seat with a back and four legs, for one person.
*He suddenly got up from his **chair**.*

chalk *noun*

Chalk is a kind of soft rock. You use small sticks of **chalk** to write or draw on a blackboard.

change *verb*
changes, changing, changed

1 When you **change** something, or when it **changes**, it becomes different.
   *The caterpillar **changed** into a butterfly.*
2 When you **change**, you put on different clothes.
   *He **changed** to go to the party.*

change *noun*

Change is the money that you get back when you pay too much for something.

chapter *noun*
chapters

A **chapter** is a part of a book.
*This book has ten **chapters**.*

character *noun*
characters

1 Your **character** is the kind of person you are.
2 A **character** is also a person in a story or a film.

charge *verb*
charges, charging, charged

If someone **charges** you an amount of money for something, they ask you to pay that amount for it.
*They **charged** us too much for our meal.*

chase *verb*
chases, chasing, chased

If you **chase** someone, you run after them and try to catch them.
*The dog **chased** the cat.*

cheap *adjective*
cheaper, cheapest

If something is **cheap**, you do not have to pay a lot of money for it.
*Milk is very **cheap** in this shop.*

check *verb*
checks, checking, checked

If you **check** something, you make sure that it is right.
*The teacher **checked** my homework.*

cheek *noun*
cheeks

Your **cheeks** are the sides of your face below your eyes.
*My **cheeks** were red.*

cheer *verb*
cheers, cheering, cheered

When people **cheer**, they shout to show that they like something.
*We all **cheered** when he won the race.*

cheerful *adjective*

Someone who is **cheerful** is happy.

cheese *noun*

Cheese is a solid food that is made from milk.

cheetah *noun*
cheetahs

A **cheetah** is a big wild cat with yellow fur and black spots.

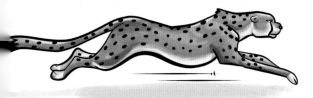

cherry *noun*
cherries

A **cherry** is a small, round fruit with a hard stone in the middle. **Cherries** are red, black, or yellow.

chew *verb*
chews, chewing, chewed

When you **chew** food, you use your teeth to break it up in your mouth before you swallow it.

chick *noun*
chicks

A **chick** is a very young bird.

chicken *noun*
chickens

1 A **chicken** is a bird that is kept on a farm for its eggs and meat.
2 **Chicken** is also the meat that comes from chickens.

child *noun*
children

A **child** is a young boy or girl.

chimney *noun*
chimneys

A **chimney** is a long pipe above a fire. Smoke from the fire goes up the **chimney** and out of the building.

chimpanzee *noun*
chimpanzees

A **chimpanzee** is a kind of small ape with dark fur.

a
b
c
d
e
f
g
h
i
j
k
l
m
n
o
p
q
r
s
t
u
v
w
x
y
z

A
B
C
D
E
F
G
H
I
J
K
L
M
N
O
P
Q
R
S
T
U
V
W
X
Y
Z

chin *noun*
chins

Your **chin** is the part of your face below your mouth.
A black beard covered his **chin**.

chip *noun*
chips

Chips or potato **chips** are thin pieces of potato fried in hot oil.

chip *verb*
chips, chipping, chipped

If you **chip** something, you break a small piece off it by accident.
I **chipped** *my tooth when I fell.*

chocolate *noun*
chocolates

Chocolate is a sweet brown food that is used to make sweets, cakes, and drinks.

choose *verb*
chooses, choosing, chose, chosen

If you **choose** something, you decide to have it.
You can **choose** *any book you want.*

chop *verb*
chops, chopping, chopped

If you **chop** something, you cut it into pieces with a knife or an axe.
He **chopped** *some wood for the fire.*

chose
⇨ Look at **choose**.
She **chose** *a dress to wear.*

chosen
⇨ Look at **choose**.
We have **chosen** *which film to watch.*

circle *noun*
circles

A **circle** is a round shape.

circus *noun*
circuses

A **circus** is a big tent where you go to see clowns and animals.

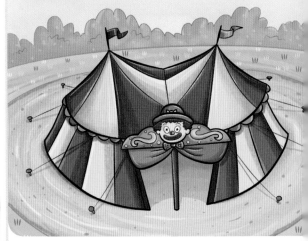

city *noun*
cities

A **city** is a very big town where a lot of people live and work.

clap *verb*
claps, clapping, clapped

When you **clap**, you hit your hands together to make a loud noise. People **clap** to show that they like something.
Everyone **clapped** *at the end of her song.*

class *noun*
classes

A **class** is a group of people who are taught together.
He is in my **class** *at school.*

classroom *noun*
classrooms

A **classroom** is a room in a school where children have lessons.

claw *noun*
claws

A bird's or an animal's **claws** are the hard, sharp, curved parts at the end of its feet.

clean *adjective*
cleaner, cleanest

Something that is **clean** does not have any dirt or marks on it.
Make sure your hands are clean.

clean *verb*
cleans, cleaning, cleaned

When you **clean** something, you take all the dirt off it.
I clean my teeth before bedtime.

clear *adjective*
clearer, clearest

1 If something is **clear**, it is easy to understand, to see, or to hear.
He gave us clear instructions on what to do.

2 If something like glass or plastic is **clear**, you can see through it.
The bottle was full of a clear liquid.

3 If a place is **clear**, it does not have anything there that you do not want.
You can cross the road when it is clear.

clear *verb*
clears, clearing, cleared

When you **clear** a place, you take away all the things you do not want there.
She cleared the table.

clever *adjective*
cleverer, cleverest

Someone who is **clever** can learn and understand things quickly.
She is very clever at maths.

cliff *noun*
cliffs

A **cliff** is a hill with one side that is very steep. **Cliffs** are often beside the sea.

climb *verb*
climbs, climbing, climbed

If you **climb** something, you move towards the top of it. You sometimes use your hands as well as your feet when you **climb**.
We climbed the tree in the garden.

cloak *noun*
cloaks

A **cloak** is a very loose coat without sleeves.

clock *noun*
clocks

A **clock** is a machine that shows you the time.

close *verb*
closes, closing, closed

When you **close** something, you shut it.
Please close the door behind you.

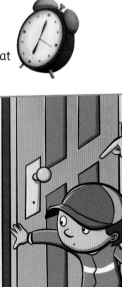

a b **c** d e f g h i j k l m n o p q r s t u v w x y z

27

A
B
C
D
E
F
G
H
I
J
K
L
M
N
O
P
Q
R
S
T
U
V
W
X
Y
Z

close *adjective*
closer, closest

If something is **close** to another thing, it is near it.
*Our house is **close** to the park.*

cloth *noun*
cloths

1 **Cloth** is material that is used to make things like clothes and curtains.

2 A **cloth** is a piece of material that you use to clean something.

clothes *noun*

Clothes are the things that people wear, for example shirts, trousers, and dresses.

cloud *noun*
clouds

A **cloud** is a white or grey shape that you see in the sky. **Clouds** are made of tiny drops of water that sometimes turn into rain.

clown *noun*
clowns

A **clown** is a person who wears funny clothes and does silly things to make people laugh.

coat *noun*
coats

You wear a **coat** on top of your other clothes when you go outside.

cobweb *noun*
cobwebs

A **cobweb** is a very thin net that a spider makes to catch insects.

coconut *noun*
coconuts

A **coconut** is a very large nut that has a very hard shell and is white inside.
Coconuts are full of a liquid called **coconut** milk.

coffee *noun*

Coffee is a drink. You make it by pouring hot water on **coffee** beans.
*Coffee beans grow on a **coffee** plant.*

coin *noun*
coins

A **coin** is a round, flat piece of metal that is used as money.

cold *adjective*
colder, coldest

1 If you are **cold**, you do not feel comfortable because you are not warm enough.
*Wear a jumper if you are **cold**.*

2 If something is **cold**, it is not hot.
*The weather is very **cold**.*

cold *noun*
colds

When you have a **cold**, you sneeze and cough a lot, and you have a sore throat.

collar *noun*
collars

1 The **collar** of a shirt or jacket is the part that goes around your neck.

2 A **collar** is also a band that goes around the neck of a dog or cat.

collect *verb*
collects, collecting, collected

1 If you **collect** things, you bring them together.
*He **collected** wood for the fire.*

2 If you **collect** someone from a place, you go there and take them away.
*Mum **collected** us from school.*

colour *noun*
colours

Red, blue and yellow are the main **colours**. You can mix them together to make other **colours**.

comb *noun*
combs

A **comb** is a flat piece of metal or plastic with very thin points that you use to make your hair tidy.

come *verb*
comes, coming, came, come

When you **come** to a place, you move towards it or arrive there.
*She **came** into the room.*

comfortable *adjective*

If something is **comfortable**, it makes you feel good.
*This is a very **comfortable** chair.*

comic *noun*
comics

A **comic** is a magazine with stories that are told in pictures.

common *adjective*

If things are **common**, you see lots of them around, or they happen often.
*Foxes are quite **common** in this area.*

compact disc *noun*
compact discs

A **compact disc** is a round, flat piece of plastic that has music or information on it. **Compact discs** are also called CDs.

competition *noun*
competitions

When you are in a **competition**, you try to show that you are the best at something.
*She won the painting **competition**.*

complete *adjective*

If something is **complete**, none of it is missing.
*He had a **complete** set of crayons.*

computer *noun*
computers

A **computer** is a machine that can store a lot of information and can work things out very quickly.
*We played games on our **computer**.*

confused *adjective*

If you are **confused**, you do not understand what is happening, or you do not know what to do.
*She was **confused** about where to go.*

consonant *noun*
consonants

A **consonant** is any letter of the alphabet that is not a, e, i, o, or u.
*The word "book" has two **consonants** in it.*

container *noun*
containers

A **container** is something that you use to keep things in, for example a box or a bottle.

a
b
c
d
e
f
g
h
i
j
k
l
m
n
o
p
q
r
s
t
u
v
w
x
y
z

29

A
B
C
D
E
F
G
H
I
J
K
L
M
N
O
P
Q
R
S
T
U
V
W
X
Y
Z

control *verb*
controls, controlling, controlled

If you **control** something, you can make it do what you want.
*I can **control** the speed by pressing this button.*

cook *verb*
cooks, cooking, cooked

When you **cook** food, you make it hot and get it ready to eat.
*Mum was **cooking** dinner.*

cooker *noun*
cookers

A **cooker** is a machine that you use to cook food.

cool *adjective*
cooler, coolest

Something that is **cool** is quite cold.
*Put the milk in the fridge to keep it **cool**.*

copy *noun*
copies

A **copy** is something that is made to look like another thing.
*I made a **copy** of the drawing.*

corn *noun*

Corn is a long vegetable. It is covered with yellow seeds that you eat.

corner *noun*
corners

A **corner** is a place where two sides join together.
*He stood at the **corner** of the street.*

correct *adjective*

If something is **correct**, there are no mistakes in it.

cost *noun*
costs

The **cost** of something is the amount of money you need to buy it.
*The **cost** of the holiday was too high.*

cot *noun*
cots

A **cot** is a bed for a baby, with high sides to stop the baby from falling out.

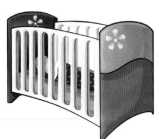

cotton *noun*

1 **Cotton** is a kind of cloth that is made from the **cotton** plant.

2 **Cotton** is also thread that you use to sew with.

cough *verb*
coughs, coughing, coughed

When you **cough**, you make air come out of your throat with a sudden, loud noise.
*The smoke made us **cough**.*

could *verb*

If you say you **could** do something, you mean that you were able to do it. **Could** comes from the word **can**.
*I **could** see through the window.*

couldn't

Couldn't is short for **could not**.
*She **couldn't** open the door.*

count *verb*
counts, counting, counted

1 When you **count**, you say numbers in order, one after the other.
*I **counted** from one to ten.*

2 When you **count** all the things in a group, you add them up to see how many there are.
*The teacher **counted** the children in the class.*

country *noun*
countries

1 A **country** is a part of the world with its own people and laws.
*He lives in a different **country**.*

2 The **country** is land that is away from towns and cities. There are farms and woods in the **country**.
*We went for a walk in the **country**.*

cousin *noun*
cousins

Your **cousin** is the son or daughter of your uncle or aunt.

cover *verb*
covers, covering, covered

If you **cover** something, you put another thing over it.
*She **covered** the table with a cloth.*

cover *noun*
covers

A **cover** is something that you put over another thing.
*Put a **cover** over the sofa to keep it clean.*

cow *noun*
cows

A **cow** is a large animal that is kept on farms because it gives milk.

crab *noun*
crabs

A **crab** is an animal with a hard shell that lives in the sea. **Crabs** have large claws on their front legs.

crack *verb*
cracks, cracking, cracked

If something **cracks**, it becomes damaged, and lines appear on the surface where it has broken.
*The window **cracked**.*

crane *noun*
cranes

1 A **crane** is a tall machine that can lift very heavy things.

2 A **crane** is also a large bird with a long neck and long legs. **Cranes** live near water.

crash *noun*
crashes

1 A **crash** is an accident when a vehicle hits something.
*There was a car **crash** outside the school.*

2 A **crash** is also a sudden, loud noise.
*He dropped the plates with a **crash**.*

crawl *verb*
crawls, crawling, crawled

When you **crawl**, you move along on your hands and knees.
*The baby **crawled** along the floor.*

crayon *noun*
crayons

Crayons are pencils or sticks of wax in different colours that you use for drawing.

cream *noun*

Cream is a thick liquid that is made from milk. You can use it in cooking or pour it over puddings.

a
b
c
d
e
f
g
h
i
j
k
l
m
n
o
p
q
r
s
t
u
v
w
x
y
z

A
B
C
D
E
F
G
H
I
J
K
L
M
N
O
P
Q
R
S
T
U
V
W
X
Y
Z

creature *noun*
creatures

A **creature** is anything that is alive, but is not a plant.
*Many **creatures** live in the forest.*

creep *verb*
creeps, creeping, crept

1 If you **creep** somewhere, you move in a very slow and quiet way.
*He **crept** up the stairs.*

2 If an animal **creeps**, it moves along close to the ground.
*The mouse **crept** across the room.*

crew *noun*
crews

A **crew** is a group of people who work together on a ship or an aeroplane.

cricket *noun*
crickets

1 **Cricket** is a game where two teams take turns to hit a ball with a bat and run up and down.

2 A **cricket** is also a small jumping insect that rubs its wings together to make a high sound.

cried
⇨ Look at **cry**.
*The baby **cried** for its mother.*

cries
⇨ Look at **cry**.
*She always **cries** at sad films.*

crocodile *noun*
crocodiles

A **crocodile** is a large reptile with a long body, a long mouth and sharp teeth. **Crocodiles'** mouths are in the shape of a letter V.

crop *noun*
crops

Crops are plants that people grow for food, for example potatoes and wheat.

cross *verb*
crosses, crossing, crossed

If you **cross** something, you go from one side of it to the other.
Cross the road where it is safe.

cross *noun*
crosses

A **cross** is a mark that you write. It looks like ✕.
*She put a **cross** beside my name.*

cross *adjective*
crosser, crossest

If you are **cross**, you feel angry about something.
*Mum was **cross** because we were late.*

crowd *noun*
crowds

A **crowd** is a lot of people together in one place.
*A big **crowd** came to see the game.*

crown *noun*
crowns

A **crown** is a circle made of gold or silver and jewels that kings and queens wear on their heads.

cry *verb*
cries, crying, cried

When you **cry**, tears come from your eyes. People **cry** when they are sad or hurt.
*The baby started to **cry**.*

cry *noun*
cries

A **cry** is a loud sound that you make with your voice.
*I heard the **cry** of a bird.*

cub *noun*
cubs

A **cub** is a young wild animal, for example a young bear or lion.

cube *noun*
cubes

A **cube** is a solid shape with six sides that are all squares.
*A dice is in the shape of a **cube**.*

cucumber *noun*
cucumbers

A **cucumber** is a long, thin, green vegetable that you eat in salads.

cuddle *verb*
cuddles, cuddling, cuddled

If you **cuddle** someone, you put your arms around them and hold them close to you.

cup *noun*
cups

A **cup** is a small, round container with a handle. You drink things like tea and coffee from a **cup**.

cupboard *noun*
cupboards

A **cupboard** is a piece of furniture with a door and shelves that you keep things in.
*The **cupboard** was full of toys.*

curl *noun*
curls

A **curl** is a piece of hair that has a curved shape.
*The girl had long, black **curls**.*

curtain *noun*
curtains

A **curtain** is a piece of cloth that you pull across a window to cover it.

curved *adjective*

If something is **curved**, it has the shape of a bent line.
*The bird had a **curved** beak.*

cushion *noun*
cushions

A **cushion** is a bag of soft material that you put on a seat to make it more comfortable.

customer *noun*
customers

A **customer** is a person who buys something in a shop.

cut *verb*
cuts, cutting, cut

1 If you **cut** something, you use a knife or scissors to divide it into pieces.
   *We **cut** the cake.*

2 If you **cut** yourself, something sharp goes through your skin and blood comes out.
   *Don't **cut** yourself on the broken glass.*

cut *noun*
cuts

A **cut** is a place on your skin where something sharp has gone through it.
*He had a **cut** on his cheek.*

a
b
c
d
e
f
g
h
i
j
k
l
m
n
o
p
q
r
s
t
u
v
w
x
y
z

Dd

dad or daddy *noun*
dads or **daddies**

Dad or **daddy** is a name for your father.

damage *verb*
damages, damaging, damaged

If you **damage** something, you break it or spoil it.
*The storm **damaged** the roof.*

damp *adjective*
damper, dampest

Something that is **damp** is a little bit wet.
*Her hair was **damp**.*

dance *verb*
dances, dancing, danced

When you **dance**, you move your body to music.

danger *noun*
dangers

If there is **danger**, something bad might happen to hurt you.
*There is a **danger** that he will fall.*

dangerous *adjective*

If something is **dangerous**, it can hurt you or kill you.
*It is **dangerous** to cross the road here.*

dark *adjective*
darker, darkest

1 When it is **dark**, there is no light or not much light.

2 A **dark** colour is not pale.
*She wore a **dark** blue skirt.*

date *noun*
dates

A **date** is the day, the month, and sometimes the year when something happens.
*What **date** is your birthday?*

daughter *noun*
daughters

Someone's **daughter** is their female child.

day *noun*
days

1 A **day** is the length of time between one midnight and the next. There are twenty-four hours in a **day**, and seven **days** in a week.
*It is three **days** until my birthday.*

2 **Day** is the time when there is light outside.
*I've been busy all **day**.*

dead *adjective*

A person, an animal, or a plant that is **dead** has stopped living.

deaf *adjective*

Someone who is **deaf** cannot hear anything, or cannot hear very well.

December *noun*

December is the month after November and before January. It has 31 days.

decide *verb*
decides, deciding, decided

When you **decide** to do something, you think about it and then choose to do it.
*She **decided** to go home.*

decorate *verb*
decorates, decorating, decorated

If you **decorate** a room, you put paint or paper on its walls.
*We **decorated** the bedroom.*

deep *adjective*
deeper, deepest

If something is **deep**, it goes down a long way.
*We dug a **deep** hole in the sand.*

deer *noun*
deer

A **deer** is a large animal that lives in forests and can run very fast. Male **deer** have big horns that look like branches on their heads.

defend *verb*
defends, defending, defended

If you **defend** someone, you keep them safe from danger.
*The soldiers **defended** the king.*

delicious *adjective*
If food is **delicious**, it tastes or smells very good.

deliver *verb*
delivers, delivering, delivered

If you **deliver** something, you take it to someone.
*Please **deliver** this letter to him.*

dentist *noun*
dentists

A **dentist** is a person whose job is to take care of people's teeth.

depth *noun*
depths

The **depth** of something is how far down it goes from its top to its bottom.
*The **depth** of the pond is two metres.*

describe *verb*
describes, describing, described

If you **describe** something, you say what it is like.
*He **described** the picture to me.*

desert *noun*
deserts

A **desert** is a large, dry area of land with almost no trees or plants. **Deserts** are very hot and are often covered with sand.

desk *noun*
desks

A **desk** is a kind of table that you sit at to write or to work.

destroy *verb*
destroys, destroying, destroyed

If you **destroy** something, you damage it so much that it cannot be used any more.
*The fire **destroyed** the house.*

a b c d e f g h i j k l m n o p q r s t u v w x y z

35

A
B
C
D
E
F
G
H
I
J
K
L
M
N
O
P
Q
R
S
T
U
V
W
X
Y
Z

diagram *noun*
diagrams

A **diagram** is a drawing that shows something in a way that is very easy to understand.
*He drew me a **diagram** of the engine.*

diamond *noun*
diamonds

1 A **diamond** is a kind of jewel that is hard, clear, and shiny.
2 A **diamond** is also a shape with four straight sides.

diary *noun*
diaries

A **diary** is a book that you use to write down things that happen to you each day.

dice *noun*
dice

A **dice** is a small cube with a different number of spots on each side. You throw **dice** in some games.

dictionary *noun*
dictionaries

A **dictionary** is a book with a list of words in it. The **dictionary** tells you what these words mean, and shows you how to spell them.

did

⇨ Look at **do**.
*I saw what you **did**.*

didn't

Didn't is short for **did not**.
*She **didn't** like the film.*

die *verb*
dies, dying, died

When a person, an animal, or a plant **dies**, they stop living.
*Plants **die** if you don't water them.*

different *adjective*

If two things are **different**, they are not like each other.
*The crayons were all in **different** colours.*

difficult *adjective*

If something is **difficult**, it is not easy to do or to understand.
*The homework was too **difficult** for us.*

dig *verb*
digs, digging, dug

If you **dig**, you make a hole in the ground.
*We **dug** a hole in the garden.*

digital *adjective*

If a machine is **digital**, it shows or sends information by using numbers.
*We have a new **digital** television.*

dinner *noun*
dinners

Dinner is the main meal of the day.

dinosaur *noun*
dinosaurs

Dinosaurs were large animals that lived a very long time ago. **Dinosaurs** were like very big lizards.

direction *noun*
directions

1 A **direction** is the way that you go to get to a place.
*My house is in this **direction**.*

2 **Directions** are words or pictures that show you how to do something, or how to get somewhere.
*He gave me **directions** to the station.*

dirt *noun*

Dirt is anything that is not clean, for example, dust or mud.
*She had **dirt** on her face.*

dirty *adjective*
dirtier, dirtiest

If something is **dirty**, it has mud, food, or other marks on it.
*The dishes were **dirty**.*

disappear *verb*
disappears, disappearing, disappeared

If something **disappears**, you cannot see it any more.
*The cat **disappeared** under the bed.*

disappointed *adjective*

If you are **disappointed**, you are sad because something you hoped for did not happen.
*I was **disappointed** that you weren't there.*

disaster *noun*
disasters

A **disaster** is something very bad that happens suddenly and that may hurt many people.

discover *verb*
discovers, discovering, discovered

When you **discover** something, you get to know about it for the first time.
*We **discovered** that he was very good at football.*

discuss *verb*
discusses, discussing, discussed

When people **discuss** something, they talk about it together.
*We **discussed** what to do next.*

disease *noun*
diseases

A **disease** is something that makes you ill.
*Measles is a **disease**.*

disguise *noun*
disguises

A **disguise** is something you wear so that people will not know who you are.

dish *noun*
dishes

A **dish** is a container that you use to cook or serve food in.

disk *noun*
disks

A **disk** is a flat piece of metal and plastic that you use in a computer to store information.

a b c d e f g h i j k l m n o p q r s t u v w x y z

A
B
C
D
E
F
G
H
I
J
K
L
M
N
O
P
Q
R
S
T
U
V
W
X
Y
Z

distance *noun*
distances

The **distance** between two things is how much space there is between them.
*Measure the **distance** between the wall and the table.*

dive *verb*
dives, diving, dived

If you **dive** into water, you jump in so that your arms and your head go in first.

divide *verb*
divides, dividing, divided

1 If you **divide** something, you make it into smaller pieces.
   ***Divide** the cake into four pieces.*

2 When you **divide** numbers, you see how many times one number goes into another number.
   *If you **divide** ten by five, you get two.*

do *verb*
does, doing, did, done

If you **do** something, you spend some time on it or finish it.
*I tried to **do** some work.*

doctor *noun*
doctors

A **doctor** is a person whose job is to help people who are ill or hurt to get better.

does
⇨ Look at **do**.
*She **does** her homework before dinner.*

doesn't
Doesn't is short for **does not**.
*He **doesn't** like carrots.*

dog *noun*
dogs

A **dog** is an animal that barks. Some **dogs** do special jobs, like helping blind people.

doing
⇨ Look at **do**.
*What are you **doing**?*

doll *noun*
dolls

A **doll** is a toy that looks like a small person or a baby.

dolphin *noun*
dolphins

A **dolphin** is an animal that lives in the sea and looks like a large fish with a long nose. **Dolphins** are very clever.

done
⇨ Look at **do**.
*She has **done** a drawing.*

donkey *noun*
donkeys

A **donkey** is an animal that looks like a small horse with long ears.

don't

Don't is short for **do not**.
*I **don't** feel well.*

door *noun*
doors

You open and close a **door** to get into a building, a room, or a cupboard.

double *adjective*

Double means two times as big, or two times as much.
*His room is **double** the size of mine.*

down

When something moves **down**, it goes from a higher place to a lower place.
*She came **down** the stairs.*

drag *verb*
drags, dragging, dragged

If you **drag** something, you pull it along the ground.
*He **dragged** his chair to the table.*

dragon *noun*
dragons

In stories, a **dragon** is a monster that has wings and can make fire come out of its mouth.

drain *verb*
drains, draining, drained

If you **drain** a liquid, you take it away by making it flow to another place.
*They **drained** the water out of the tunnel.*

drank

⇨ Look at **drink**.
*She **drank** a bottle of water.*

draw *verb*
draws, drawing, drew, drawn

When you **draw**, you use pens, pencils, or crayons to make a picture.
*He likes to **draw** animals.*

drawer *noun*
drawers

A **drawer** is a box that fits inside a piece of furniture. You can pull it out and put things in it.

drawing *noun*
drawings

A **drawing** is a picture you make with pens, pencils, or crayons.

drawn

⇨ Look at **draw**.
*I have **drawn** my house.*

dream *noun*
dreams

A **dream** is something you see and hear in your mind while you are sleeping.
*I had a **dream** about winning the prize.*

dress *noun*
dresses

A **dress** is something a girl or a woman can wear. It covers the body and part of the legs.
*She wore a yellow **dress**.*

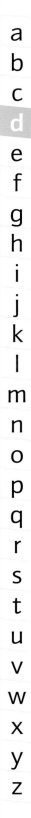

A
B
C
D
E
F
G
H
I
J
K
L
M
N
O
P
Q
R
S
T
U
V
W
X
Y
Z

dress *verb*
dresses, dressing, dressed

When you **dress**, you put on clothes.
*He **dressed** quickly because he was late.*

drew
⇨ Look at **draw**.
*She **drew** a picture of a horse.*

drink *verb*
drinks, drinking, drank, drunk

When you **drink**, you swallow liquid.
*Mum **drinks** a lot of coffee.*

drip *verb*
drips, dripping, dripped

When liquid **drips**, a small amount of it falls from somewhere.
*Water **dripped** from the roof.*

drive *verb*
drives, driving, drove, driven

When someone **drives** a vehicle, they make it go where they want.
*He knows how to **drive** a car.*

drop *verb*
drops, dropping, dropped

If you **drop** something, you let it fall.
*I **dropped** a plate on the floor.*

drove
⇨ Look at **drive**.
*We **drove** to the shops.*

drown *verb*
drowns, drowning, drowned

If someone **drowns**, they die because their face is below water and they cannot breathe.

drum *noun*
drums

A **drum** is an instrument that you hit with sticks or with your hands to make music.

drunk
⇨ Look at **drink**.
*Have you **drunk** all the milk?*

dry *adjective*
drier, driest

If something is **dry**, there is no water in it or on it.
*My clothes are **dry**.*

duck *noun*
ducks

A **duck** is a bird that lives near water and can swim. **Ducks** have large flat beaks.

dug
⇨ Look at **dig**.
*We **dug** a hole in the sand.*

dull *adjective*
duller, dullest

1 Something that is **dull** is not interesting.
   *That was a very **dull** book.*

2 A **dull** colour is not bright.
   *He wore a **dull** green jacket.*

dust *noun*

Dust is tiny pieces of dry dirt that looks like powder.
*The table was covered in **dust**.*

Ee

each

Each means every one.
*He gave **each** of us a book.*

eagle *noun*
eagles

An **eagle** is a large bird with a curved beak and sharp claws. **Eagles** eat small animals.

ear *noun*
ears

Your **ears** are the two parts of your body that you hear sounds with.
*He whispered something in her **ear**.*

early *adjective*
earlier, earliest

1 If you are **early**, you arrive before the time that you were expected to come.
   *She was too **early** for the party.*
2 **Early** also means near the first part of something.
   *I got up **early** in the morning.*

earn *verb*
earns, earning, earned

If you **earn** money, you work to get it.
*He **earned** some money washing the car.*

earth *noun*

1 The **Earth** is the planet that we live on.
2 **Earth** is also the soil that plants grow in.

earthquake *noun*
earthquakes

When there is an **earthquake**, the ground shakes and buildings often fall down.

east *noun*

The **east** is the direction that is in front of you when you are looking towards the place where the sun rises.

easy *adjective*
easier, easiest

If something is **easy**, you can do it or understand it without having to try very much.
*These sums are **easy**.*

eat *verb*
eats, eating, ate, eaten

When you **eat**, you chew and swallow food.
*She **eats** too many sweets.*

echo *noun*
echoes

An **echo** is a sound that you hear again because it bounces off something solid and then comes back.
*We heard the **echo** of our voices in the cave.*

a b c d e f g h i j k l m n o p q r s t u v w x y z

A
B
C
D
E
F
G
H
I
J
K
L
M
N
O
P
Q
R
S
T
U
V
W
X
Y
Z

edge *noun*
edges

The **edge** of something is the part along the end or side of it.
*She stood at the **edge** of the pond.*

effect *noun*
effects

An **effect** is something that happens because of another thing.
*The flood was an **effect** of all the rain.*

effort *noun*
efforts

If you make an **effort** to do something, you have to work a lot to do it.
*She made an **effort** to win the race.*

egg *noun*
eggs

Baby birds, insects, and some other animals live in **eggs** until they are big enough to come out and be born. People often eat hens' **eggs** as food.

eight *noun*
Eight is the number **8**.

elbow *noun*
elbows

Your **elbow** is the part in the middle of your arm where it bends.
*She put her **elbows** on the table.*

electricity *noun*

Electricity is a kind of energy that is used to make light, to make things hot, and to make machines work.

elephant *noun*
elephants

An **elephant** is a very large, grey animal with big ears, a long nose called a trunk, and two long, curved teeth called tusks.

eleven *noun*
Eleven is the number .

email or **e-mail** *noun*

An **email** is a message like a letter that you send from one computer to another.
*I got an **email** from my cousin.*

empty *adjective*
emptier, emptiest

If something is **empty**, there is nothing inside it.
*The bottle was **empty**.*

encyclopedia *noun*
encyclopedias

An **encyclopedia** is a book that gives you information about many different things.

end *noun*
ends

The **end** of something is the last part of it.
*He told me the **end** of the story.*

enemy *noun*
enemies

If someone is your **enemy**, they hate you and want to hurt you.

energy *noun*

1 If you have **energy**, you have the strength to move around a lot and do things.
*He has the **energy** to run for miles.*

2 **Energy** is also the power that makes machines work.
*The lamp gets its **energy** from the sun.*

engine *noun*
engines

1 An **engine** is a machine that makes things like cars and planes move.

2 An **engine** is also the front part of a train that pulls it along.

enjoy *verb*
enjoys, enjoying, enjoyed

If you **enjoy** something, you like doing it.
*I **enjoy** reading.*

enormous *adjective*

Something that is **enormous** is very big.
*Whales are **enormous**.*

enough

If you have **enough** of something, you have as much as you need.
*I don't have **enough** money to buy both books.*

enter *verb*
enters, entering, entered

When you **enter** a place, you go into it.

entrance *noun*
entrances

The **entrance** of a place is the way you get into it.
*We found the **entrance** to the tunnel.*

envelope *noun*
envelopes

An **envelope** is a paper cover that you put a letter or a card into before you send it to someone.

environment *noun*

The **environment** is the land, water, and air around us.
*We must try to protect the **environment**.*

equal *adjective*

If two things are **equal**, they are the same in size, number, or amount.
*Mix **equal** amounts of milk and water.*

equipment *noun*

Equipment is all the things that you need to do something.
*He put his football **equipment** in his bag.*

escape *verb*
escapes, escaping, escaped

If a person or an animal **escapes**, they get away from somewhere.
*My guinea pig **escaped** from its cage.*

even *adjective*

1 An **even** number is a number that you can divide by two, with nothing left over.
*Four is an **even** number.*

2 Something that is **even** is flat and smooth.
*The path was straight and **even**.*

a
b
c
d
e
f
g
h
i
j
k
l
m
n
o
p
q
r
s
t
u
v
w
x
y
z

A
B
C
D
E
F
G
H
I
J
K
L
M
N
O
P
Q
R
S
T
U
V
W
X
Y
Z

evening *noun*
evenings

The **evening** is the part of each day between the end of the afternoon and the time when people usually go to bed.

ever

Ever means at any time.
*Have you **ever** seen anything like it?*

every *adjective*

You use **every** to mean all the people or things in a group.
***Every** pupil in the school was there.*

everybody

Everybody means all the people in a group, or all the people in the world.
***Everybody** likes him.*

everyone

Everyone means all the people in a group, or all the people in the world.
***Everyone** knows who she is.*

everything

Everything means all of something.
*He told me **everything** that happened.*

everywhere

Everywhere means in every place.
*I looked **everywhere** for my keys.*

example *noun*
examples

An **example** is something that you use to show what other things in the same group are like.
*Here is an **example** of my drawings.*

excellent *adjective*

Something that is **excellent** is very good.
*It was an **excellent** film.*

excited *adjective*

If you are **excited**, you are very happy about something and you keep thinking about it.
*He was very **excited** about going to the beach.*

excuse *noun*
excuses

An **excuse** is a reason that you give to explain why you did something.
*She had a good **excuse** for being late.*

exercise *noun*
exercises

1 When you do **exercise**, you move your body so that you can keep healthy and strong.
   *Running and swimming are both good **exercise**.*

2 An **exercise** is also something you do to practise what you have learnt.
   *We did a maths **exercise**.*

exit *noun*
exits

The **exit** of a building is the door you use to get out of it.
*We left by the nearest **exit**.*

expect *verb*
expects, expecting, expected

If you **expect** something to happen, you think that it will happen.
*I **expect** that he will come.*

expensive *adjective*

If something is **expensive**, you need a lot of money to buy it.

explain *verb*
explains, explaining, explained

If you **explain** something, you talk about it so that people can understand it.
*He **explained** to me how the machine worked.*

explode *verb*
explodes, exploding, exploded

If something **explodes**, it bursts with a very loud noise.

explore *verb*
explores, exploring, explored

If you **explore** a place, you look around it to see what it is like.
*We **explored** the old castle.*

extinct *adjective*

If an animal or a plant is **extinct**, there are none of them alive any more.
*Dinosaurs are **extinct**.*

extra *adjective*

Extra means more than the usual amount.
*I wore an **extra** jumper because it was cold.*

eye *noun*
eyes

Your **eyes** are the parts of your body that you see with.
*I opened my **eyes** and looked.*

face *noun*
faces

Your **face** is the front part of your head.
*She has a beautiful **face**.*

fact *noun*
facts

A **fact** is something that you know is true.

factory *noun*
factories

A **factory** is a large building where people use machines to make things.
*He works in a **factory** that makes computers.*

fail *verb*
fails, failing, failed

If you **fail**, you try to do something but you cannot do it.
*She **failed** to find her lost keys.*

fair *adjective*
fairer, fairest

1 If something is **fair**, it seems right because it is the same for everyone.
*It's not **fair** – he's got more than me!*

2 **Fair** hair is pale yellow in colour.

A
B
C
D
E
F
G
H
I
J
K
L
M
N
O
P
Q
R
S
T
U
V
W
X
Y
Z

fairy *noun*
fairies

In stories, **fairies** are tiny creatures with wings who can do magic.

fall *verb*
falls, falling, fell, fallen

If a person or thing **falls**, they move towards the ground suddenly by accident.
*He **fell** off his bike.*

fallen
⇨ Look at **fall**.
*An apple had **fallen** from the tree.*

family *noun*
families

A **family** is a group of people made up of parents and their children. Aunts and uncles, cousins, grandmothers, and grandfathers are also part of your **family**.

famous *adjective*

If someone is **famous**, a lot of people know who they are.
*She wants to be rich and **famous**.*

far
farther, farthest

If something is **far** away, it is a long way away.
His house was far away.

farm *noun*
farms

A **farm** is a piece of land with buildings on it where people grow crops and keep animals.

farmer *noun*
farmers

A **farmer** is a person who grows crops and keeps animals on a farm.

fast *adjective*
faster, fastest

Something that is **fast** can move quickly.
*This car is very **fast**.*

fasten *verb*
fastens, fastening, fastened

When you **fasten** something, you close it up.
*She **fastened** the buttons on her coat.*

fat *adjective*
fatter, fattest

Someone who is **fat** has a big, round body.

father *noun*
fathers

A **father** is a man who has a child.

fault *noun*
faults

If something bad is your **fault**, you made it happen.
*It's my **fault** that we were late.*

favourite *adjective*

Your **favourite** person or thing is the one you like best.
*My **favourite** food is cheese.*

fear *noun*

Fear is the way you feel when you think that something bad is going to happen to you.
*She shook with **fear**.*

feast *noun*
feasts

A **feast** is a large and special meal for a lot of people.

feather *noun*
feathers

Feathers are the soft, light things that cover a bird's body. They keep the bird warm and help it to fly.

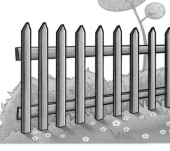

February *noun*

February is the month after January and before March. It usually has 28 days, but once every four years, it has 29 days.

feed *verb*
feeds, feeding, fed

If you **feed** a person or an animal, you give them food.
*I **feed** my cat twice a day.*

feel *verb*
feels, feeling, felt

1   The way you **feel**, for example happy or sad, or cold or tired, is how you are at the time.
*I **feel** very upset.*
2   If you **feel** something, you touch it with your hand to see what it is like.
***Feel** how soft these feathers are.*

feet

⇨ Look at **foot**.
*Don't put your **feet** on the chair.*

fell

⇨ Look at **fall**.
*She **fell** and hurt her knee.*

felt

⇨ Look at **feel**.
*I **felt** angry.*

female *adjective*

A **female** person or animal could become a mother.

fence *noun*
fences

A **fence** is a wall made of wood or metal that goes round a piece of land.
*There is a **fence** round the garden.*

fetch *verb*
fetches, fetching, fetched

If you **fetch** something, you go to where it is and bring it back.
*He **fetched** a towel from the bathroom.*

fever *noun*
fevers

If you have a **fever** when you are ill, your body is too hot.

few
fewer, fewest

A **few** means some, but not many.
*She gave me a **few** sweets.*

a
b
c
d
e
f
g
h
i
j
k
l
m
n
o
p
q
r
s
t
u
v
w
x
y
z

A
B
C
D
E
F
G
H
I
J
K
L
M
N
O
P
Q
R
S
T
U
V
W
X
Y
Z

field *noun*
fields

A **field** is a piece of land where people grow crops or keep animals.

fierce *adjective*
fiercer, fiercest

A **fierce** animal is very angry and might attack you.
*That dog looks very **fierce**.*

fight *verb*
fights, fighting, fought

When people **fight**, they try to hurt each other.
*Two boys started to **fight** in the playground.*

fill *verb*
fills, filling, filled

If you **fill** something, you put so much into it that you cannot get any more in.
*She **filled** her cup with tea.*

film *noun*
films

A **film** is a story told in moving pictures that you watch on a screen.

fin *noun*
fins

A **fin** is one of the thin, flat parts on a fish's body that help it to swim.

find *verb*
finds, finding, found

If you **find** something that has been lost, you see it after you have been looking for it.
*I can't **find** my shoes.*

fine *adjective*
finer, finest

1 If you say that you are **fine**, you mean that you are well or happy.
   *I feel **fine** now.*

2 Something that is **fine** is very thin.
   *She sewed the cloth with **fine** thread.*

3 When the weather is **fine**, it is dry and sunny.
   *It is a **fine** day.*

finger *noun*
fingers

Your **fingers** are the long thin parts at the end of each hand.
*She put the ring on her **finger**.*

finish *verb*
finishes, finishing, finished

When you **finish** something, you come to the end of it.
*I **finished** my homework.*

fire *noun*
fires

Fire is the hot, bright flames that come from something that is burning.
*The **fire** destroyed the forest.*

fire engine *noun*
fire engines

A **fire engine** is a large truck that carries people and equipment to stop fires.

firework *noun*
fireworks

Fireworks are things that make a loud bang or flashes of bright colour when they are burned.

firm *adjective*
firmer, firmest

Something that is **firm** is hard, and is not easy to bend.

first *adjective*

If a person or thing is **first**, they come before all the others.
*January is the **first** month of the year.*

fish *noun*
fish, fishes

A **fish** is an animal that lives in water. **Fish** have fins to help them swim.

fit *verb*
fits, fitting, fitted

If something **fits** you, it is the right size and shape for you.
*These shoes don't **fit** me.*

five *noun*

Five is the number **5** .

fix *verb*
fixes, fixing, fixed

1 If you **fix** something that is broken, you mend it.
   *He **fixed** the radio.*

2 If you **fix** something to another thing, you join them together.
   *She **fixed** the shelf to the wall.*

flag *noun*
flags

A **flag** is a piece of cloth with a pattern on it. Each country of the world has its own **flag**.

flame *noun*
flames

A **flame** is the hot, bright light that comes from a fire.
*The **flames** almost burned her fingers.*

flash *noun*
flashes

A **flash** is a sudden bright light.
*There was a **flash** of lightning.*

flat *adjective*
flatter, flattest

If something is **flat**, it is smooth and does not have any lumps.
*Lay the painting on a **flat** surface until it is dry.*

flavour *noun*
flavours

The **flavour** of food is the taste that it has.
*They had ice cream in lots of **flavours**.*

flew

⇨ Look at **fly**.
*An aeroplane **flew** across the sky.*

flies

⇨ Look at **fly**.
*A bird **flies** by moving its wings.*

float *verb*
floats, floating, floated

1 If something **floats** in a liquid, it stays on top of it.
   *The boat **floated** on the water.*

2 If something **floats** in the air, it moves slowly through it.
   *A balloon **floated** over our heads.*

a
b
c
d
e
f
g
h
i
j
k
l
m
n
o
p
q
r
s
t
u
v
w
x
y
z

49

flock *noun*
flocks

A **flock** is the name for a group of birds or sheep.

flood *noun*
floods

If there is a **flood**, a lot of water covers land that is usually dry.

*We couldn't get to school because of the **flood**.*

floor *noun*
floors

1 A **floor** is the part of a room that you walk on.

*There were carpets on the **floor**.*

2 A **floor** of a building is all the rooms in it that are at the same height.

*Our house is on the first **floor**.*

flour *noun*

Flour is a powder made from wheat that is used to make bread and cakes.

flow *verb*
flows, flowing, flowed

If something **flows**, it moves along in a steady way and does not stop.

*The river **flowed** through the forest.*

flower *noun*
flowers

A **flower** is the part of a plant that makes seeds. **Flowers** often have bright colours and a nice smell.

flown

⇨ Look at **fly**.

*The birds have all **flown** away.*

flu *noun*

If you have **flu**, you feel as if you have a very bad cold, and your body aches.

fly *verb*
flies, flying, flew, flown

When a bird or aeroplane **flies**, it moves through the air.

fly *noun*
flies

A **fly** is a small insect with two thin, clear wings.

fog *noun*

Fog is a thick cloud that is close to the ground. It is hard to see through it.

fold *verb*
folds, folding, folded

If you **fold** something, you bend it so that one part of it goes over another.

*He **folded** the letter and put it in the envelope.*

follow *verb*
follows, following, followed

If you **follow** someone, you go along behind them.

*We **followed** him up the stairs.*

food *noun*
foods

Food is what people and animals eat.

foot *noun*
feet

Your **feet** are the parts of your body that are at the ends of your legs, and that you stand on.
*Stand with one **foot** in front of the other.*

football *noun*
footballs

1 **Football** is a game played by two teams of eleven people who kick a ball and try to score goals by getting the ball into a net.

2 A **football** is the ball that you use to play football.

forehead *noun*
foreheads

Your **forehead** is the part of your face that is between your hair and your eyes.
*She had a bruise on her **forehead**.*

forest *noun*
forests

A **forest** is a place where a lot of trees grow close together.

forever

If something goes on **forever**, it never comes to an end.
*The film seemed to go on **forever**.*

forgave
⇨ Look at **forgive**.
*She **forgave** her brother for spoiling her drawing.*

forget *verb*
forgets, forgetting, forgot, forgotten

If you **forget** something, you do not remember it.
*Don't **forget** to lock the door.*

forgive *verb*
forgives, forgiving, forgave, forgiven

If you **forgive** someone who has done something bad, you stop being angry with them.
*Please **forgive** me for being late.*

forgot
⇨ Look at **forget**.
*She **forgot** to bring any money.*

forgotten
⇨ Look at **forget**.
*I have **forgotten** my keys.*

fork *noun*
forks

A **fork** is a tool with three or four thin, sharp points that you use to eat food with.

fortnight *noun*
fortnights

A **fortnight** is two weeks.

forwards

If you move **forwards**, you move towards the front.
*They ran backwards and **forwards** trying to catch the ball.*

a
b
c
d
e
f
g
h
i
j
k
l
m
n
o
p
q
r
s
t
u
v
w
x
y
z

51

A
B
C
D
E
F
G
H
I
J
K
L
M
N
O
P
Q
R
S
T
U
V
W
X
Y
Z

fought
⇨ Look at **fight**.
*The knights **fought** with swords.*

found
⇨ Look at **find**.
*She **found** her lost dog.*

four *noun*
Four is the number **4**.

fox *noun*
foxes

A **fox** is an animal that looks like a dog with red fur and a long, thick tail.

fraction *noun*
fractions

A **fraction** is a part of a whole number.
*A half and a quarter are both **fractions**.*

frame *noun*
frames

A **frame** is a piece of wood, metal or plastic that fits around the edge of a picture, a window, or a door.

frame

freckles *noun*
Freckles are light brown spots that some people have on their skin.
*His face was covered with **freckles**.*

free *adjective*
freer, freest

1 If something is **free**, you can have it without paying any money for it.
*If you buy a cup of coffee, you get a **free** cake.*

2 If you are **free**, you can do what you like or go where you like.
*You are **free** to come here any time.*

freeze *verb*
freezes, freezing, froze, frozen

1 When water **freezes**, it is so cold that it becomes ice.

2 If you **freeze** food, you make it very cold so that it will not go bad.

fresh *adjective*
fresher, freshest

1 If food is **fresh**, it has been picked or made a short time ago.
*Eat some **fresh** fruit every day.*

2 **Fresh** water has no salt in it. The water in rivers is **fresh**.

3 **Fresh** air is clean and cool.

Friday *noun*
Fridays

Friday is the day after Thursday and before Saturday.
*He went home on **Friday**.*

fridge *noun*
fridges

A **fridge** is a cupboard that uses electricity to keep food cold and fresh.
*Put the butter in the **fridge**.*

fried
➡ Look at **fry**.
*She **fried** some eggs.*

friend *noun*
friends
A **friend** is someone you know and like, and who likes you too.

friendly *adjective*
friendlier, friendliest
If someone is **friendly**, they like to meet other people, and are nice to them.

frighten *verb*
frightens, frightening, frightened
If something **frightens** you, it makes you feel afraid.
*Loud noises **frighten** her.*

frog *noun*
frogs
A **frog** is a small animal with smooth skin, big eyes, and long back legs that it uses for jumping. **Frogs** live near water.

front *noun*
fronts
The **front** of something is the part that comes first or the part that you usually see first.
*She stood at the **front** of the queue.*

frost *noun*
Frost is ice that looks like white powder. It covers things outside when the weather is very cold.

frown *verb*
frowns, frowning, frowned
When you **frown**, lines appear on your forehead because you are cross or because you are thinking about something.

froze
➡ Look at **freeze**.
*It was so cold that the lake **froze**.*

frozen
➡ Look at **freeze**.
*The water had **frozen** into ice.*

fruit *noun*
fruits
Fruit is the part of a plant or a tree that has the seeds in it. You can eat many **fruits**, for example apples, bananas, and strawberries.

fry *verb*
fries, frying, fried
When you **fry** food, you cook it in hot oil or butter.
Fry the onions until they are brown.

full *adjective*
fuller, fullest
If something is **full**, it has so much in it that it cannot hold any more.
*The bottle is **full**.*

a b c d e f g h i j k l m n o p q r s t u v w x y z

A
B
C
D
E
F
G
H
I
J
K
L
M
N
O
P
Q
R
S
T
U
V
W
X
Y
Z

fun *noun*

When you have **fun**, you enjoy doing something and you feel happy.
*They had **fun** at the beach.*

funny *adjective*
funnier, funniest

1 If something is **funny**, it makes you laugh.
*He told me a **funny** joke.*

2 **Funny** also means strange.
*The car is making a **funny** noise.*

fur *noun*

Fur is the soft hair that covers the bodies of many animals.
*Pandas have black and white **fur**.*

furniture *noun*

Furniture is the name for all the big things, for example tables, chairs, or beds, that people have in their houses.
*We bought new **furniture** for the bedroom.*

future *noun*

The **future** is the time that will come after the present time.
*In the **future**, people will travel to other planets.*

gale *noun*
gales

A **gale** is a very strong wind.

game *noun*
games

1 A **game** is something you play that has rules, for example football.

2 Children also play a **game** when they pretend to be other people.
*We played a **game** of pirates.*

gap *noun*
gaps

A **gap** is a space between two things.
*There was a **gap** between the curtains.*

garage *noun*
garages

1 A **garage** is a building where you keep a car.

2 A **garage** is also a place where you can get your car repaired.

garden *noun*
gardens

A **garden** is a piece of land near a house where people can grow grass, flowers, and vegetables.

gas *noun*
gases

A **gas** is anything, for example air, that is not solid or a liquid.

gate *noun*
gates

A **gate** is a kind of door in a wall, a fence, or a hedge.

gave

⇨ Look at **give**.
*She **gave** me a present.*

gentle *adjective*
gentler, gentlest

If you are **gentle**, you are careful and not rough.
*Be **gentle** when you hold the baby.*

get *verb*
gets, getting, got

1 You can use **get** to mean the same as "become".
   *We should go before it **gets** dark.*

2 If you **get** some where, you arrive there.
   *He **got** home at noon.*

3 If you **get** something, someone gives it to you.
   *I **got** a bike for my birthday.*

4 If you **get** something, you go to where it is and bring it back.
   *He went to **get** a cup of coffee.*

ghost *noun*
ghosts

A **ghost** is a dead person who some people think they can see and hear.

giant *adjective*

Something that is **giant** is very large.
*They watched the film on a **giant** TV screen.*

giraffe *noun*
giraffes

A **giraffe** is a very tall animal with a long neck, long legs, and dark spots on its body.

girl *noun*
girls

A **girl** is a child or a young person who is a female.

give *verb*
gives, giving, gave, given

If you **give** someone something, you let them have it to keep.
*We always **give** our mother flowers on her birthday.*

glad *adjective*
gladder, gladdest

If you are **glad**, you are happy about something.
*I'm **glad** you can come to my party.*

glass *noun*
glasses

1 **Glass** is a hard, clear material that is used to make things like windows and bottles. It is quite easy to break **glass**.
   *The salad was in a **glass** bowl.*

2 A **glass** is also a container made from glass that you can drink out of.
   *He filled his **glass** with milk.*

glasses *noun*

Glasses are two pieces of plastic or glass in a frame that people wear in front of their eyes to help them to see better.

a
b
c
d
e
f
g
h
i
j
k
l
m
n
o
p
q
r
s
t
u
v
w
x
y
z

A
B
C
D
E
F
G
H
I
J
K
L
M
N
O
P
Q
R
S
T
U
V
W
X
Y
Z

glove *noun*
gloves

Gloves are things that you wear over your hands to keep them warm. **Gloves** have one part for your thumb and one for all your fingers.

glue *noun*

You use **glue** to stick things together.

go *verb*
goes, going, went, gone

1 If you **go** somewhere, you move there from another place.
Can we go to the park?

2 If you say that something is **going** to happen, you mean that it will happen.
He's going to leave soon.

goal *noun*
goals

In games like football, the **goal** is the place that you try to get the ball in to, to score a point.

goat *noun*
goats

A **goat** is an animal about the size of a sheep. **Goats** have horns, and hair on their chin that looks like a beard.

gold *noun*

Gold is a valuable, yellow metal that is used to make things like rings and necklaces, and also coins.

goldfish *noun*
goldfish

A **goldfish** is a small orange fish that people often keep as a pet.

gone

⇨ Look at **go**.
She has gone home.

good *adjective*
better, best

1 If you say that something is **good**, you like it.
That was a good film.

2 If you are **good**, you behave well.
Be good while I am out.

3 If you are **good** at something, you do it well.
She is good at drawing.

goodbye

You say **goodbye** to someone when one of you is going away.

good night

You say **good night** to someone late in the evening before you go home or go to bed.

goose *noun*
geese

A **goose** is a large bird with a long neck that lives near water.

gorilla *noun*
gorillas

A **gorilla** is a large, strong animal with long arms, black fur, and a black face.

got

⇨ Look at **get**.
They soon got tired of the game.

grain *noun*
grains

1 A **grain** is the seed of a cereal plant, for example rice or wheat.
2 A **grain** of something, for example sand or salt, is a tiny piece of it.

gram *noun*
grams

A **gram** is used for measuring how heavy things are.
*There are about 400 **grams** of jam in this jar.*

grandfather *noun*
grandfathers

Your **grandfather** is your father's father or your mother's father.

grandmother *noun*
grandmothers

Your **grandmother** is your father's mother or your mother's mother.

grape *noun*
grapes

A **grape** is a small, round, green or purple fruit that grows in bunches.

grapefruit *noun*
grapefruits

A **grapefruit** is a large, round, yellow fruit with a sour taste.

graph *noun*
graphs

In maths, a **graph** is a picture that uses lines or shapes to show numbers.

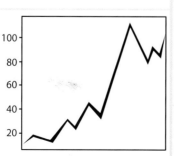

grass *noun*
grasses

Grass is a green plant with very thin leaves that cover the ground in fields and gardens.

great *adjective*
greater, greatest

1 **Great** means very large.
   *The king lived in a **great** palace.*
2 **Great** also means very important.
   *The computer was a **great** invention.*
3 If you say that something is **great**, you mean that it is very good.
   *We had a **great** time.*

greedy *adjective*
greedier, greediest

If someone is **greedy**, they want to have more of something than they need.
*He was so **greedy** that he ate the whole cake.*

green *noun/adjective*

Green is the colour of grass or leaves.
*Her dress is **green**.*

grew

⇨ Look at **grow**.
*The tree **grew** to a great height.*

grey *noun*

Grey is a mixture of black and white, like the colour of clouds when rain is falling.

ground *noun*

The **ground** is the earth or other surface that you walk on outside.

a b c d e f **g** h i j k l m n o p q r s t u v w x y z

A
B
C
D
E
F
G
H
I
J
K
L
M
N
O
P
Q
R
S
T
U
V
W
X
Y
Z

group *noun*
groups

A **group** is a number of people or things that are together, or that belong together.

grow *verb*
grows, growing, grew, grown

When something **grows**, it gets bigger.
*The puppy **grew** into a huge dog.*

guess *verb*
guesses, guessing, guessed

If you **guess**, you say what you think is true about something, but you do not really know if you are right.
*Can you **guess** how old he is?*

guinea pig *noun*
guinea pigs

A **guinea pig** is a small animal with fur and no tail that people often keep as a pet.

guitar *noun*
guitars

A **guitar** is an instrument with strings that you play by pressing the strings with one hand and pulling them with the other hand.

had
➡ Look at **have**.
*We **had** a nice time.*

hadn't
Hadn't is short for **had not**.
*I **hadn't** seen them for a long time.*

hair *noun*
Hair is the soft, fine threads that grow on your head and on the bodies of many animals.
*I wash my **hair** every night.*

half *noun*
halves

A **half** is one of two equal parts that make up a whole thing.
*We each had **half** of the cake.*

halves
➡ Look at **half**.
*Cut the apples into **halves**.*

hamster *noun*
hamsters

A **hamster** is a small animal that looks like a fat mouse with a short tail. People often keep **hamsters** as pets.

hand *noun*
hands

Your **hands** are the parts of your body that are at the ends of your arms, and that you use to hold things. A **hand** has four fingers and a thumb.
*I put my **hand** in my pocket and took out the letter.*

handle *noun*
handles

1 A **handle** is something that is joined to a door, a window, or a drawer, that you use to open and close it.
*She pulled the **handle** of the drawer.*

2 A **handle** is also the part of something, for example a tool or a bag, that you use to hold it.
*Hold the knife by its **handle**.*

hang *verb*
hangs, hanging, hung

If you **hang** something somewhere, you fix the top of it to something so that it does not touch the ground.
*She **hung** her coat on a peg.*

happen *verb*
happens, happening, happened

When something **happens**, it takes place.
*What's **happening** in the playground?*

happy *adjective*
happier, happiest

When you are **happy**, you feel pleased about something.

hard *adjective*
harder, hardest

1 Something that is **hard** is solid, and it is not easy to bend it or break it.
*The glass broke on the **hard** floor.*

2 If something is **hard**, you have to try a lot to do it or to understand it.
*These sums are quite **hard**.*

has

⇨ Look at **have**.
*He **has** a sister.*

hasn't

Hasn't is short for **has not**.
*She **hasn't** anything to do.*

hat *noun*
hats

A **hat** is something that you can wear on your head.

hatch *verb*
hatches, hatching, hatched

When a baby bird or other animal **hatches**, it comes out of its egg by breaking the shell. You can also say that the egg **hatches**.

hate *verb*
hates, hating, hated

If you **hate** a person or a thing, you feel that you do not like them at all.
*I **hate** onions.*

have *verb*
has, having, had

1 If you **have** something, it belongs to you.
*Do you **have** any pets?*

2 When you **have** something, you feel it, or it happens to you.
*I **have** a bad cold.*

a
b
c
d
e
f
g
h
i
j
k
l
m
n
o
p
q
r
s
t
u
v
w
x
y
z

A
B
C
D
E
F
G
H
I
J
K
L
M
N
O
P
Q
R
S
T
U
V
W
X
Y
Z

haven't

Haven't is short for **have not**.
*I **haven't** any chocolate left.*

hay *noun*

Hay is dry grass that is used to feed animals.

head *noun*
heads

1 Your **head** is the part of your body at the top that has your eyes, ears, nose, mouth, and brain in it.
*The ball hit him on the **head**.*

2 The **head** of something is the person who is its leader.
*He is the **head** of the school.*

heal *verb*
heals, healing, healed

If something like a broken bone **heals**, it gets better.

healthy *adjective*
healthier, healthiest

1 Someone who is **healthy** is well and strong and is not often ill.
*People need exercise to stay **healthy**.*

2 Something that is **healthy** is good for you.
*Eat **healthy** food like fruit and vegetables.*

hear *verb*
hears, hearing, heard

When you **hear** a sound, you notice it through your ears.
*I **heard** a dog barking.*

heart *noun*
hearts

Your **heart** is the part inside you that makes the blood move around your body.
*His **heart** was going fast.*

heavy *adjective*
heavier, heaviest

Something that is **heavy** weighs a lot.
*This bag is very **heavy**.*

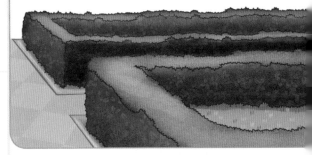

he'd

1 **He'd** is short for **he had**.
***He'd** seen it before.*

2 **He'd** is also short for **he would**.
***He'd** like them.*

hedge *noun.*
hedges

A **hedge** is a row of bushes growing close together that makes a kind of wall. You often see **hedges** around fields.

heel *noun*
heels

Your **heels** are the parts of your feet at the back, below your ankles.
*He dragged his **heels** along the ground.*

height *noun*
heights

Your **height** is how tall you are.
*We all measured our **heights**.*

held

⟹ Look at **hold**.

*Mum **held** my hand as we crossed the road.*

helicopter *noun*
helicopters

A **helicopter** is a small aircraft with long blades on top that go round very quickly. **Helicopters** can fly straight up and down and stay in one place in the air.

he'll

He'll is short for **he will**.
He'll come back soon.

hello

You say **hello** to someone when you meet them.

help *verb*
helps, helping, helped

If you **help** someone, you make it easier for them to do something.
*He **helped** me with my homework.*

hen *noun*
hens

A **hen** is a chicken that is a female. People often eat **hens'** eggs as food.

her

You use **her** to talk about a woman or a girl, or to say that something belongs to a woman or a girl.
*I gave **her** back **her** pen.*

herd *noun*
herds

A **herd** is a large group of animals that lives together.
*We saw a **herd** of deer in the forest.*

here

Here means the place where you are.
*Come and sit **here**.*

hers

You use **hers** to say that something belongs to a woman or a girl.
*She said that the bag was **hers**.*

herself

You use **herself** when you want to say that something a woman or a girl does has an effect on her.
*She pulled **herself** out of the water.*

he's

He's is short for **he is**.
He's six years old.

hexagon *noun*
hexagons

A **hexagon** is a shape with six straight sides.

hid

⟹ Look at **hide**.
*They **hid** in the cupboard.*

a
b
c
d
e
f
g
h
i
j
k
l
m
n
o
p
q
r
s
t
u
v
w
x
y
z

A
B
C
D
E
F
G
H
I
J
K
L
M
N
O
P
Q
R
S
T
U
V
W
X
Y
Z

hidden

⇨ Look at **hide**.
*He was **hidden** under the bed.*

hide *verb*
hides, hiding, hid, hidden

1 If you **hide** something, you put it where no one can see it or find it.
   *He **hid** his bike behind the wall.*

2 If you **hide** what you feel, you do not let people know about it.
   *She tried to **hide** how angry she was.*

high *adjective*
higher, highest

1 Something that is **high** is tall or is a long way above the ground.
   *There was a **high** wall around the house.*

2 **High** also means great in amount or strength.
   *They charged us a **high** price.*

3 A **high** sound or voice goes up a long way.
   *She spoke in a **high** voice.*

hill *noun*
hills

A **hill** is a piece of land that is higher than the land around it. **Hills** are not as high as mountains.

him

You use **him** to talk about a man or a boy.
*We met **him** at the station.*

himself

You use **himself** when you want to say that something a man or a boy does has an effect on him.
*He fell and hurt **himself**.*

hippopotamus *noun*
hippopotamuses or **hippopotami**

A **hippopotamus** is a large animal with short legs and thick skin that lives near rivers.

his

You use **his** to say that something belongs to a man or a boy.
*He showed me **his** new football.*

history *noun*

History is the story of what has happened in the past.

hit *verb*
hits, hitting, hit

If you **hit** something, you touch it with a lot of strength.
*She **hit** the ball with the bat.*

hive *noun*
hives

A **hive** is a place where bees live.

hold *verb*
holds, holding, held

1 When you **hold** something, you have it in your hands or your arms.
*She **held** the baby in her arms.*

2 If something **holds** an amount of something, then that is how much it has room for inside.
*The theatre **holds** 400 people.*

hole *noun*
holes

A **hole** is a gap or a hollow place in something.
*We dug a **hole** in the ground.*

holiday *noun*
holidays

A **holiday** is a time when you do not need to work or go to school.

hollow *adjective*

Something that is **hollow** has an empty space inside it.
*The owl's nest was in a **hollow** tree.*

home *noun*
homes

Your **home** is the place where you live.
*We stayed at **home** and watched TV.*

homework *noun*

Homework is something like sums that a teacher gives you to work on at home.

honest *adjective*

If someone is **honest**, they do not tell lies, and you can believe what they say.

honey *noun*

Honey is a sweet, very thick liquid that is made by bees. You can eat **honey** on bread.

hoof *noun*
hooves

A **hoof** is the hard part of a horse's foot. Deer and cows also have **hooves**.

hop *verb*
hops, hopping, hopped

1 If you **hop**, you jump on one foot.

2 When animals or birds **hop**, they jump with two feet together.

hope *verb*
hopes, hoping, hoped

If you **hope** that something will happen, you want it to happen.
*I **hope** you feel better soon.*

horn *noun*
horns

1 A **horn** is one of the hard bones with sharp points that grow out of some animals' heads. Goats and bulls have **horns**.

2 A **horn** is also an instrument that you blow into to make music.

horrible *adjective*

If something is **horrible**, it is very nasty.
*There was a **horrible** smell.*

a b c d e f g h i j k l m n o p q r s t u v w x y z

A
B
C
D
E
F
G
H
I
J
K
L
M
N
O
P
Q
R
S
T
U
V
W
X
Y
Z

horse *noun*
horses

A **horse** is a large animal with a long tail and four legs. People ride on **horses** or use them to pull things along.

hospital *noun*
hospitals

A **hospital** is a building where doctors and nurses care for people who are ill or hurt.

hot *adjective*
hotter, hottest

If something is **hot**, it is very warm.
*Don't touch the plate – it's **hot**.*

hour *noun*
hours

An **hour** is used for measuring time. There are sixty minutes in an **hour**, and twenty-four **hours** in a day.

house *noun*
houses

A **house** is a building where people live.
*Come to my **house** for dinner.*

how

1 You use the word **how** when you ask about the way that something happens or the way that you do something.
   How do you spell your name?

2 You also use **how** when you ask about an amount.
   How many people were at the party?

hug *verb*
hugs, hugging, hugged

When you **hug** someone, you put your arms around them and hold them close to you.
*She **hugged** me as we said goodbye.*

huge *adjective*

Something that is **huge** is very big.
*Elephants are **huge** animals.*

human *adjective*

Something that is **human** is to do with people, and not animals or machines.
*There are over 200 bones in the **human** body.*

hundred *noun*

A **hundred** is the number 100.

hung

⇨ Look at **hang**.
*He **hung** from the bars.*

hungry *adjective*
hungrier, hungriest

If you are **hungry**, you want to eat something.

hunt verb
hunts, hunting, hunted

1 When animals **hunt**, they chase another animal to kill it for food.
*The lions **hunted** a zebra.*

2 If you **hunt** for something, you try to find it.
*I **hunted** for my keys.*

hurry verb
hurries, hurrying, hurried

If you **hurry**, you move quickly or do something quickly.
*We'll be late if we don't **hurry**.*

hurt verb
hurts, hurting, hurt

If you **hurt** someone or something, you make them feel pain.
*I fell over and **hurt** my leg yesterday.*

husband noun
husbands

A woman's **husband** is the man she is married to.

hut noun
huts

A **hut** is a small building with one or two rooms. **Huts** are made of wood, mud, or grass.

hutch noun
hutches

A **hutch** is a kind of cage made of wood and wire, where people keep rabbits and other small pets.

Ii

I

You use **I** to talk about yourself.
I like chocolate.

ice noun

Ice is water that has frozen. It is very cold and hard.
*The ground was covered with **ice**.*

ice cream noun

Ice cream is a very cold, sweet food that is made from frozen milk or cream.

icicle noun
icicles

An **icicle** is a long piece of ice with a point at the end that hangs down from something. **Icicles** are made from dripping water that has frozen.

I'd

1 **I'd** is short for **I had**.
I'd been there before.

2 **I'd** is also short for **I would**.
I'd like to go to the zoo.

a
b
c
d
e
f
g
h
i
j
k
l
m
n
o
p
q
r
s
t
u
v
w
x
y
z

idea *noun*
ideas

An **idea** is something new that you have thought of.
*He had an **idea** for a story.*

ill *adjective*
When you are **ill**, you do not feel well.
*She is too **ill** to go to school.*

I'll
I'll is short for **I will**.
I'll come back tomorrow.

illness *noun*
illnesses

If you have an **illness**, you do not feel well.
*He has just had a very bad **illness**.*

I'm
I'm is short for **I am**.
I'm hungry.

imagine *verb*
imagines, imagining, imagined

If you **imagine** something, you make a picture of it in your mind.
Imagine that you are a cat.

immediately
If you do something **immediately**, you do it now.
*Stop that noise **immediately**!*

important *adjective*
1 If something is **important**, people care about it and think about it a lot.
*It is **important** not to tell lies.*

2 If someone is **important**, people pay a lot of attention to what they say and do.
*She is a very **important** person.*

impossible *adjective*
If something is **impossible**, it cannot be done, or it cannot happen.
*It is **impossible** to see in the dark.*

in
1 **In** means not outside.
*The juice is **in** the fridge.*

2 You also use **in** to say when something happens.
*He was born **in** March.*

inch *noun*
inches

An **inch** is used for measuring the length of something. There are about two and half centimetres in an **inch**.

indoors
If you are **indoors**, you are inside a building.

information *noun*
Information about something is facts that tell you about it.
*I need some **information** about birds.*

ink *noun*

Ink is a liquid that you use to write or print with. Pens have **ink** inside them.

insect *noun*
insects

An **insect** is a small animal with six legs, for example a bee or a beetle. Many **insects** have wings and can fly.

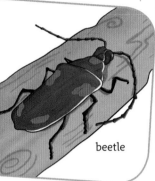

beetle

inside

1 If something is **inside** another thing, it is in it.
*There was a letter **inside** the envelope.*

2 **Inside** also means indoors.
*He went **inside** and locked the door.*

instructions *noun*

Instructions are words or pictures that tell you how to do something.
*Here are the **instructions** for building the tent.*

instrument *noun*
instruments

1 An **instrument** is a tool that you use to do something.
*The doctor used an **instrument** to look in my ears.*

2 An **instrument** is also something, for example a piano or a guitar, that you use to make music.
*He plays three **instruments**.*

intelligent *adjective*

If a person is **intelligent**, they are able to understand and learn things quickly.

interesting *adjective*

If something is **interesting**, you want to know more about it.

Internet *noun*

The **Internet** is something that joins a computer to other computers all over the world. You send emails using the **Internet**.

interrupt *verb*
interrupts, interrupting, interrupted

If you **interrupt** someone, you say or do something that makes them stop in the middle of what they are doing.
*Don't **interrupt** the teacher when she's talking.*

invention *noun*
inventions

An **invention** is something that someone has made, and that nobody has ever thought of or made before.
*His new **invention** is a car that can fly.*

invisible *adjective*

If something is **invisible**, you cannot see it.

invite *verb*
invites, inviting, invited

If you **invite** someone to something, for example a party, you ask them to come to it.

a
b
c
d
e
f
g
h
i
j
k
l
m
n
o
p
q
r
s
t
u
v
w
x
y
z

A
B
C
D
E
F
G
H
I
J
K
L
M
N
O
P
Q
R
S
T
U
V
W
X
Y
Z

iron *noun*
irons

1 **Iron** is a strong, hard, grey metal.

2 An **iron** is a piece of equipment with a flat bottom that gets hot. You move the bottom over clothes to make them smooth.

is
⇨ Look at **be**.
*She **is** six years old.*

island *noun*
islands

An **island** is a piece of land that has water all around it.

isn't
Isn't is short for **is not**.
*He **isn't** very happy.*

it
You use **it** to talk about a thing or an animal.
*This is a good book – have you read **it**?*

its
You use **its** to say that something belongs to a thing or an animal.
*The lion lifted **its** head.*

it's
It's is short for **it is**.
It's one o'clock.

I've
I've is short for **I have**.
I've been playing football.

Jj

jacket *noun*
jackets

A **jacket** is a short coat.

jam *noun*

Jam is a soft, sweet food that is made from fruit and sugar.
*I love strawberry **jam** on my bread.*

January *noun*

January is the month after December and before February. It has 31 days.

jar *noun*
jars

A **jar** is a glass container with a lid that is used for storing food.
*Make sure you put the lid back on the **jar**.*

jaw *noun*
jaws

Your **jaws** are the top and bottom bones of your mouth.

jaw

jeans *noun*

Jeans are blue trousers with pockets at the front and back.
*Everyone on the trip wore **jeans** and a bright T-shirt.*

jelly *noun*

Jelly is a clear, sweet food that is solid but soft.
*We had birthday cake, then **jelly** and ice cream.*

jet *noun*
jets

A **jet** is a plane that flies very fast.

jewel *noun*
jewels

1 A **jewel** is a valuable stone, like a diamond.

2 **Jewels** are things made with valuable stones, that you wear to decorate your body.
*She put the **jewels** in the box and turned the key.*

jigsaw *noun*
jigsaws

A **jigsaw** is a picture on cardboard that has been cut up into pieces. You have to fit them together again.
*The children put the last pieces in the **jigsaw**.*

job *noun*
jobs

A **job** is the work that a person does to earn money.
*My sister wants to get a **job**.*

join *verb*
joins, joining, joined

1 If you **join** a group of people, you become one of the group.
*Come and **join** the music group after school on Mondays.*

2 When things **join**, or you **join** them, they come together.
*They **joined** hands and danced.*

joke *noun*
jokes

A **joke** is something that someone says to make you laugh.
*Grandfather always tells us **jokes** after dinner.*

journey *noun*
journeys

When you make a **journey**, you travel from one place to another.
*It was a difficult **journey** that took several days.*

jug *noun*
jugs

A **jug** is a container with a handle. You use a **jug** for pouring liquids.
*There is a **jug** of cold water on the table.*

juice *noun*
juices

Juice is the liquid from a fruit or vegetable.
*He had a large glass of fresh orange **juice**.*

a b c d e f g h i j k l m n o p q r s t u v w x y z

July *noun*

July is the month after June and before August. It has 31 days.

jump *verb*
jumps, jumping, jumped

When you **jump**, you bend your knees and push yourself into the air.
*I **jumped** over the fence.*

jumper *noun*
jumpers

You wear a **jumper** to keep yourself warm. It has sleeves and covers the top half of your body.

June *noun*

June is the month after May and before July. It has 30 days.

jungle *noun*
jungles

A **jungle** is a thick, wet forest in a hot country.
*They followed the path deep into the **jungle**.*

just

If you **just** did something, you did it a very short time ago.
*We **just** got home after an awful journey.*

kangaroo *noun*
kangaroos

A **kangaroo** is a large Australian animal that carries its babies in a pocket on its stomach.

keen *adjective*
keener, keenest

If you are **keen**, you want to do something very much.
*Everyone was **keen** to help.*

keep *verb*
keeps, keeping, kept

1 If someone **keeps** away from a place, they do not go near it.
   Keep away from the road.

2 If someone **keeps** still or warm, they stay like that.
   *We lit a fire to **keep** warm.*
   *"**Keep** still!"*

3 If you **keep** doing something, you do it many times or you do it some more.
   *I **keep** forgetting to take my umbrella.*

4 When you **keep** something, you store it somewhere.
   *She **kept** her money under the bed.*

kennel *noun*
kennels

A **kennel** is a small house where a dog can sleep.

kept
⇨ Look at **keep**.
*She **kept** her head down.*

kettle *noun*
kettles

A **kettle** is a metal container with a lid and a handle, that you use for boiling water.
*Mum put the **kettle** on and made some tea.*

key *noun*
keys

1 A **key** is a piece of metal that opens or closes a lock.
*They put the **key** in the door and it opened.*

2 The **keys** on a computer or instrument are the buttons that you press on it.
*Press the "Enter" **key**.*

kick *verb*
kicks, kicking, kicked

If you **kick** something, you hit it with your foot.
*He **kicked** the ball really hard.*

kid *noun*
kids

A **kid** is a child.
*They have three **kids**.*

kill *verb*
kills, killing, killed

To **kill** a living thing is to make it die.
*The earthquake **killed** 62 people.*

kilogram *noun*
kilograms

A **kilogram** is used for measuring how heavy things are. There are 1,000 grams in a **kilogram**.
*The box weighs 4.5 **kilograms**.*

kilometre *noun*
kilometres

A **kilometre** is used for measuring distance. There are 1,000 metres in a **kilometre**, which is about 0.62 miles.

kind *noun*
kinds

A **kind** of thing is a type or sort of that thing.
*What **kind** of car is that?*

kind *adjective*
kinder, kindest

Someone who is **kind** is friendly and helps you.
*Thank you for being so **kind** to me.*

king *noun*
kings

A **king** is a man who rules a country.
*We saw the **king** and queen arriving.*

kiss *verb*
kisses, kissing, kissed

If you **kiss** someone, you touch them with your lips.
*We **kissed** goodbye at the airport.*

kitchen *noun*
kitchens

A **kitchen** is a room that is used for cooking.

a b c d e f g h i j k l m n o p q r s t u v w x y z

A
B
C
D
E
F
G
H
I
J
K
L
M
N
O
P
Q
R
S
T
U
V
W
X
Y
Z

kite *noun*
kites

A **kite** is a toy that you fly in the wind at the end of a long string.
*We went to the beach to fly **kites**.*

kitten *noun*
kittens

A **kitten** is a very young cat.

knee *noun*
knees

Your **knee** is the part in the middle of your leg where it bends.
*I fell over and hurt my **knee**.*

kneel *verb*
kneels, kneeling, knelt

When you **kneel**, you bend your legs and rest on one or both of your knees.
*She **knelt** down beside the bed.*

knew
⇨ Look at **know**.
*I **knew** all the kids at the party.*

knife *noun*
knives

A **knife** is a sharp metal tool that you use to cut things.
*I finished and put down my **knife** and fork.*

knight *noun*
knights

In the past, a **knight** was a soldier who rode a horse.

knit *verb*
knits, knitting, knitted

If you **knit** something, you make it from a long piece of wool by using two special sticks.
*My grandmother sat **knitting**.*

knives
⇨ Look at **knife**.
*We put all the **knives** away in their box.*

knock *verb*
knocks, knocking, knocked

If you **knock** on something, you hit it to make a noise.
*She went to his house and **knocked** on the door.*

knot *noun*
knots

You make a **knot** when you tie two pieces of something together.
*He picked up the rope and tied a **knot** in it.*

know *verb*
knows, knowing, knew, known

1 If you **know** something, you have that information in your mind.
*You should **know** the answer to that question.*

2 If you **know** a person, you have met them and spoken to them.
*I didn't **know** any of the other people in the class.*

label *noun*
labels

A **label** is a small note on something that gives you information about it.
*The prices are on the **labels**.*

lace *noun*
laces

1   **Lace** is a pretty cloth that has patterns of holes in it.
    *Her dress was dark blue with a white **lace** collar.*

2   **Laces** are like pieces of string for fastening shoes.
    *He put on his shoes and tied the **laces**.*

ladder *noun*
ladders

A **ladder** is a set of steps that you can move around. You use it for reaching high places.
*He climbed the **ladder** to see over the wall.*

lady *noun*
ladies

You can use **lady** to talk about a woman in a polite way.
*She's a very nice old **lady**.*

ladybird *noun*
ladybirds

A **ladybird** is a small round beetle that has red wings with black spots.

laid
⇨ Look at **lay**.
*She **laid** out the food on the table.*

lain
⇨ Look at **lie**.
*He had **lain** awake all night, worrying.*

lake *noun*
lakes

A **lake** is an area of water with land around it.

lamb *noun*
lambs

A **lamb** is a young sheep.

lamp *noun*
lamps

A **lamp** is a light that uses electricity, oil or gas.
*She turned on the **lamp** by her bed.*

land *noun*

Land is an area of ground.
*This is good farm **land**.*

land *verb*
lands, landing, landed

When something **lands**, it comes down to the ground after moving through the air.
*The ball **landed** in the middle of the road.*

lane *noun*
lanes

A **lane** is a narrow road, usually in the country.

a b c d e f g h i j k l m n o p q r s t u v w x y z

73

A
B
C
D
E
F
G
H
I
J
K
L
M
N
O
P
Q
R
S
T
U
V
W
X
Y
Z

language *noun*
languages

A **language** is a set of words that the people of a country use in talking or writing.
*The English **language** has over 500,000 words.*

lap *noun*
laps

Your **lap** is the flat area on top of your thighs when you are sitting down.
*The boy sat on his dad's **lap**.*

large *adjective*
larger, largest

A **large** thing or person is big or bigger than usual.
*This fish lives in **large** rivers and lakes.*

last *adjective*

1 The **last** thing is the one before this one.
   *In the **last** lesson, we looked at some flowers.*
2 The **last** thing or person comes after all the others.
   *I read the **last** three pages of the chapter.*

late
later, latest

1 **Late** means near the end of a period of time.
   *It was **late** in the afternoon.*
2 **Late** also means after the proper time.
   *We arrived **late** for our class.*

laugh *verb*
laughs, laughing, laughed

When you **laugh**, you smile and make a sound because something is funny.
*The boys all **laughed** at his joke.*

law *noun*
laws

A **law** is a rule that tells people what they may or may not do in a country.

lawn *noun*
lawns

A **lawn** is an area of short grass.
*Let's sit on the **lawn**.*

lay *verb*
lays, laying, laid

1 When you **lay** something somewhere, you put it down so that it lies there.
   ***Lay** the dishes on the table.*
2 When a bird **lays** an egg, it pushes an egg out of its body.

lay

⇨ Look at **lie**.
*We **lay** on the grass and looked at the sky.*

layer *noun*
layers

A **layer** is something that covers a surface, or that lies between two other things.
*A **layer** of new snow covered the street.*

lazy *adjective*
lazier, laziest

A **lazy** person does not like working.
*He was too **lazy** to read the whole book.*

lead *verb*
leads, leading, led

If you **lead** someone to a place, you take them there.
*I took his hand and started to **lead** him into the house.*

lead *noun*

If you are in the **lead** in a race or competition, you are winning.
*Our team was in the **lead** after ten minutes.*

lead *noun*

Lead is a soft, grey, heavy metal.

leader *noun*
leaders

The **leader** of a group of people or a country is the person who is in charge of it.
*Your team **leaders** have your instructions.*

leaf *noun*
leaves

The **leaves** of a plant are the parts that are flat, thin, and usually green.
*A dry, brown **leaf** floated on the water.*

lean *verb*
leans, leaning, leant or **leaned**

When you **lean**, you bend your body from your waist.
*She **leant** forwards and looked at me again.*

leap *verb*
leaps, leaping, leapt or **leaped**

If you **leap**, you jump a long way or very high.
*He **leaped** in the air and waved his hands.*

learn *verb*
learns, learning, learnt or **learned**

When you **learn** something, you get to know it or how to do it.
*When did you **learn** to swim?*

leather *noun*

Leather is the skin of some animals that you can use for making things.
*Is your jacket made of real **leather**?*

leave *verb*
leaves, leaving, left

1 When you **leave** a place, you go away from it.
  *Our bus **leaves** in an hour.*

2 If you **leave** something somewhere, you do not bring it with you.
  *I **left** my bags in the car.*

leaves

⇨ Look at **leaf**.
*The **leaves** are beginning to turn brown.*

led

⇨ Look at **lead**.
*The woman **led** me through the door into her office.*

left *noun*

The **left** is one side of something. For example, on a page, English writing begins on the **left**.
*The school is on the **left** at the end of the road.*

left

⇨ Look at **leave**.
*The teacher suddenly **left** the room.*

a
b
c
d
e
f
g
h
i
j
k
l
m
n
o
p
q
r
s
t
u
v
w
x
y
z

leg *noun*
legs

1 A person's or animal's **legs** are the long parts of their body that they use for walking and standing.
Stand with your arms stretched out and your legs apart.

2 The **legs** of a table or chair are the long parts that it stands on.
One of the legs is loose.

leg

lemon *noun*
lemons

A **lemon** is a yellow fruit with very sour juice.

lend *verb*
lends, lending, lent

If you **lend** someone something, you give it to them for a period of time and then they give it back to you.
Will you lend me your pen?

length *noun*
lengths

The **length** of something is how long it is from one end to the other.
The table is about a metre in length.

lent
⇨ Look at **lend**.
I lent her two books to read on holiday.

leopard *noun*
leopards

A **leopard** is a large, wild cat. **Leopards** have yellow fur with black spots, and live in Africa and Asia.

less *adjective*
Less means a smaller amount.
I am trying to spend less money on sweets.

lesson *noun*
lessons

A **lesson** is a period of time when someone teaches you something.
My sister has a piano lesson every Monday.

let *verb*
lets, letting, let

1 If you **let** someone do something, you allow them to do it.

2 You can say **let's** when you want someone to do something with you. **Let's** is short for **let us**.
Let's go!

letter *noun*
letters

1 A **letter** is a message on paper that you post to someone.
I received a letter from a friend.

2 **Letters** are shapes that you write to make words.
The children practised writing the letters in class.

lettuce *noun*
lettuces

A **lettuce** is a vegetable with large green leaves that you eat in salads.

library *noun*
libraries

A **library** is a place where you can go to read or borrow books.
I'm going to the library to look for a book about whales.

lick *verb*
licks, licking, licked

If you **lick** something, you move your tongue over it.
Lick the stamp before you put it on the envelope.

lid *noun*
lids

A **lid** is the top of a container that you can remove.
She lifted the lid of the box.

lie *verb*
lies, lying, lay, lain

When you **lie** somewhere, your body is flat, and you are not standing or sitting.
Lie on the bed and close your eyes for a while.

lie *noun*
lies

A **lie** is something you say that is not true.
You told me a lie!

life *noun*
lives

Your **life** is the period of time when you are alive.
I want to live here for the rest of my life.

lift *verb*
lifts, lifting, lifted

When you **lift** something, you take it and move it up.
He lifted the bag on to his shoulder.

light *noun*
lights

1 **Light** is the bright energy that comes from the sun, that lets you see things.
   A little light comes into the room through the thin curtains.

2 A **light** is something like a lamp, that allows you to see.
   There was only one small light in the room.

light *adjective*
lighter, lightest

1 If a place is **light**, it is bright because of the sun or lamps.
   It gets light at about 6 o'clock here.

2 Something that is **light** is not heavy.
   The chair is quite light so we can move it if we want to.

3 A **light** colour is pale.
   His shirt was light blue.

light *verb*
lights, lighting, lit

When you **light** a fire, it starts burning.
We used a whole box of matches to light the fire.

lightning *noun*

Lightning is the very bright flashes of light in the sky in a storm.
There was thunder and lightning and big black clouds in the sky.

like

1 If things or people are **like** each other, they are almost the same.
   He's very funny, like my uncle.

2 You say what something or someone is **like** when you are talking about how they seem to you.
   "What was the party like?"—"Oh it was great!"

like *verb*
likes, liking, liked

If you **like** something, you think it is nice or interesting.
Do you like swimming?

A
B
C
D
E
F
G
H
I
J
K
L
M
N
O
P
Q
R
S
T
U
V
W
X
Y
Z

line *noun*
lines

A **line** is a long, thin mark or shape.
*Draw a **line** at the bottom of the page.*

lion *noun*
lions

A **lion** is a large wild cat that lives in Africa. **Lions** have yellow fur, and male **lions** have long hair on their head and neck.

lip *noun*
lips

Your **lips** are the edges of your mouth.
*He bit his **lip**.*

liquid *noun*
liquids

A **liquid** is something that you can pour. Water and oil are **liquids**.
*The bottle is full of clear **liquid**.*

list *noun*
lists

A **list** is a set of names or other things that you write one below the other.
*There are six names on the **list**.*

listen *verb*
listens, listening, listened

If you **listen** to something, you hear it and give it your attention.
*He's **listening** to the radio.*

lit
⇨ Look at **light**.
*He took a match and **lit** the candle.*

litre *noun*
litres

A **litre** is used for measuring liquid.

litter *noun*
Litter is rubbish that people drop in the street.
*Please don't drop any **litter**.*

little *adjective*
littler, littlest

A person or thing that is **little** is small in size.
*They live in a **little** house.*

live *verb*
lives, living, lived

1 You **live** in the place where your home is.
   *Where do you **live**?*

2 To **live** means to be alive.
   *We all need water to **live**.*

lives
⇨ Look at **life**.
*Their **lives** were changed.*

lizard *noun*
lizards

A **lizard** is a small reptile with a long tail and rough skin.

load *verb*
loads, loading, loaded

If you **load** a vehicle, you put something on it.
*We finished **loading** the bags on to the lorry.*

loaf *noun*
loaves

A **loaf** is bread that you cut into slices.
He bought a loaf of bread and some cheese.

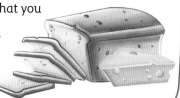

lock *verb*
locks, locking, locked

When you **lock** a door, you close it with a key.
Are you sure you locked the front door?

log *noun*
logs

A **log** is a thick piece of wood from a tree.
We sat around a log fire.

lolly *noun*
lollies

A **lolly** is a sweet or ice cream on a stick.

long *adjective*
longer, longest

1 Something that is **long** takes a lot of time.
   The afternoon lessons seemed very long.

2 Something that is **long** measures a great distance from one end to the other.
   There is a long table in the middle of the kitchen.

look *verb*
looks, looking, looked

1 When you **look** at something, you turn your eyes so that you can see it.
   I looked at the clock and yawned.

2 You use **look** when you describe how a person seems.
   The little girl looked sad.

loose *adjective*
looser, loosest

1 Something that is **loose** moves when it should not.
   One of the table legs is loose.

2 **Loose** clothes are rather large and are not tight.
   Wear loose, comfortable clothes when you do the exercises.

lorry *noun*
lorries

A **lorry** is a large vehicle for moving things by road.

lose *verb*
loses, losing, lost

1 If you **lose** a game, you do not win it.
   Our team lost the match by one point.

2 If you **lose** something, you do not know where it is.
   I've lost my keys.

lost *adjective*

If you are **lost**, you do not know where you are.
I suddenly knew that I was lost.

lot or lots

A **lot** of something, or **lots** of something, is a large amount of it.
He drank lots of milk.

loud *adjective*
louder, loudest

A **loud** noise is a very big sound.
The music was very loud.

a
b
c
d
e
f
g
h
i
j
k
l
m
n
o
p
q
r
s
t
u
v
w
x
y
z

A
B
C
D
E
F
G
H
I
J
K
L
M
N
O
P
Q
R
S
T
U
V
W
X
Y
Z

love *verb*
loves, loving, loved

1 If you **love** someone, you care very much about them.
2 If you **love** something, you like it very much.
*We both **love** football.*

lovely *adjective*
lovelier, loveliest

A **lovely** thing or person is very beautiful or very nice.
*I thought she looked **lovely**.*

low *adjective*
lower, lowest

1 Something that is **low** is close to the ground.
*There is a **low** fence around the house.*
2 A **low** number is a small number.
*The price was very **low**.*

lucky *adjective*
luckier, luckiest

Someone who is **lucky** enjoys good things that people don't expect to happen.
*He was **lucky** to win the competition.*

lump *noun*
lumps

A **lump** is a solid piece of something.
*There was a bowl full of **lumps** of sugar.*

lunch *noun*
lunches

Lunch is the meal that you have in the middle of the day.

lying
⇨ Look at **lie**.
*There was a man **lying** on the ground.*

machine *noun*
machines

A **machine** is a piece of equipment that uses electricity or an engine to do something.
*I left a message on the answering **machine**.*

made
⇨ Look at **make.**
*Mum **made** me a big birthday cake.*

magazine *noun*
magazines

A **magazine** is a thin book with stories and pictures in it.
*I get my favourite **magazine** every Thursday.*

magic *noun*

In stories, **magic** is a special power that allows you to do impossible things.
*By **magic**, the man turned to stone.*

magnet *noun*
magnets

A **magnet** is a piece of metal that attracts iron towards it.

main *adjective*

The **main** thing is the most important one.
*That's the **main** reason I want it.*

make *verb*
makes, making, made

1 If you **make** something, you put it together or build it from other things.
*She **makes** all her own clothes.*

2 You can use **make** to show that a person does or says something.
*He **made** a phone call.*

3 If you **make** a person do something, they must do it.
*Mum **made** me clean the bathroom.*

male *adjective*

A **male** person or animal could become a father.
*All of the pupils were **male**.*

mammal *noun*
mammals

Mammals are animals that feed their babies with milk.
*Some **mammals**, like whales, live in the sea.*

man *noun*
men

A **man** is an adult male person.
*The book is for both **men** and women.*

manage *verb*
manages, managing, managed

If you **manage** something, you control it.
*He **managed** the bank for 20 years.*

many *adjective*

If there are **many** people or things, there are a lot of them.
*Does he have **many** friends?*

map *noun*
maps

A **map** is a drawing of an area from above. It shows where the roads, rivers and railways are.
*You can see the park beside this road on the **map**.*

March *noun*

March is the month after February and before April. It has 31 days.

mark *noun*
marks

1 A **mark** is a small dirty area on a surface.
*I can't get this **mark** off my shirt.*

2 A **mark** is a shape that you write or draw.
*He made a few **marks** with his pen.*

market *noun*
markets

A **market** is a place where people buy and sell things.
*There's a **market** in the town centre every Saturday morning.*

marmalade *noun*

Marmalade is jam that is made from oranges.

marry *verb*
marries, marrying, married

When a man and a woman **marry**, they become husband and wife.

mask *noun*
masks

A **mask** is something that you wear over your face to protect or hide it.

A
B
C
D
E
F
G
H
I
J
K
L
M
N
O
P
Q
R
S
T
U
V
W
X
Y
Z

mat *noun*
mats

A **mat** is a small piece of cloth, wood, or plastic that you put on a table to protect it.
*I put my glass on a red **mat**.*

match *noun*
matches

1 A **match** is a small, thin stick that makes a flame when you rub it on a rough surface.
*She lit a **match** and held it up to the candle.*

2 A **match** is a game of football, cricket, or some other sport.
*We won all our **matches** last year.*

match *verb*
matches, matching, matched

If one thing **matches** another, they look good together.
*Do these shoes **match** my dress?*

material *noun*
materials

1 **Material** is cloth.
*Her skirt was made from thick black **material**.*

2 A **material** is what something is made of, like rock, glass or plastic.
*Wax is a soft **material**.*

maths *noun*

If you learn **maths**, you learn about numbers, shapes, and amounts.

matter *verb*
matters, mattered

If something **matters** to you, it is important.
*Never mind, it doesn't **matter**.*

may *verb*

1 If you **may** do something, it is possible that you will do it.
*I **may** come back next year.*

2 If you **may** do something, you can do it because someone allows you to do it.
*Please **may** I leave the room?*

May *noun*

May is the month after April and before June. It has 31 days.

me

You use **me** when you are talking about yourself.
*Can you hear **me**?*

meal *noun*
meals

A **meal** is food that you eat at one time. Breakfast, lunch and dinner are **meals**.
*She sat next to me for every **meal**.*

mean *verb*
means, meaning, meant

1 If you ask what something **means**, you want to understand it.
*What does this word **mean**?*

2 If you **mean** what you are saying, it is not a joke.
*He says he loves her, and I think he **means** it.*

3 If you **mean** to do something, it is not an accident.
*I didn't **mean** to drop the cup.*

mean *adjective*
meaner, meanest

Someone who is **mean** is not nice to other people.
*He was sorry for being **mean** to her.*

measles *noun*

Measles is an illness that gives you a fever and red spots on your skin.

measure *verb*
measures, measuring, measured

If you **measure** something, you find its size.
*First **measure** the length of the table.*

meat *noun*

Meat is the part of an animal that people cook and eat.
*I don't eat **meat** or fish.*

medicine *noun*

Medicine is something that you swallow to make you better when you are ill.
*The **medicine** saved his life.*

meet *verb*
meets, meeting, met

If you **meet** someone, you see them and you talk to them.
*I **met** my friends in town today.*

melon *noun*
melons

A **melon** is a large, soft, sweet fruit with a hard green or yellow skin.
*We ate slices of **melon**.*

melt *verb*
melts, melting, melted

When something **melts**, it changes from a solid to a liquid as it becomes warmer.
Melt the chocolate in a bowl.

memory *noun*
memories

1 Your **memory** is the part of your mind that remembers things.
*He has a very good **memory** for numbers.*

2 A **memory** is something you remember about the past.
*They discussed their **memories** of their school days.*

men
⇨ Look at **man**.
*He ordered his **men** to stop.*

mend *verb*
mends, mending, mended

If you **mend** something that is broken, you repair it.
*They **mended** the hole in the roof.*

mess *noun*

If something is a **mess**, it is not neat.
*After the party, the house was a **mess**.*

message *noun*
messages

A **message** is a piece of information that you send someone.
*I got emails and **messages** from friends all over the world.*

messy *adjective*
messier, messiest

A person or thing that is **messy** is not neat.
*His writing is rather **messy**.*

met
⇨ Look at **meet**.
*We **met** when we were on holiday.*

a b c d e f g h i j k l **m** n o p q r s t u v w x y z

metal *noun*
metals

Metal is a hard material that melts when it gets very hot.
*Gold, iron and lead are different kinds of **metal**.*

metre *noun*
metres

A **metre** is used for measuring distances or how long things are.
*The hole in the ground is about one and a half **metres** across.*

mice
⇨ Look at **mouse**.
*You can hear the **mice** under the floor.*

midday *noun*

Midday is twelve o'clock in the middle of the day.
*At **midday** everyone had lunch.*

middle *noun*
middles

The **middle** of something is the part that is the same distance from each edge or end.
*We stood in the **middle** of the room.*

midnight *noun*

Midnight is twelve o'clock at night.
*They went to bed after **midnight**.*

might *verb*

You use **might** when something is possible.
*He **might** win the race.*

mile *noun*
miles

A **mile** is used for measuring distance.
*They drove 600 **miles** across the desert.*

milk *noun*

Milk is the white liquid that all baby mammals get from their mothers. People also drink **milk** that farmers get from cows.
*They make cheese from goat's and sheep's **milk** too.*

millilitre *noun*
millilitres

A **millilitre** is used for measuring liquid.
There are 1,000 **millilitres** in a litre.
*I gave him the medicine with a 5 **millilitre** spoon.*

millimetre *noun*
millimetres

A **millimetre** is used for measuring how long things are.
There are 1,000 **millimetres** in a metre.
*The small insect was a few **millimetres** long.*

mind *noun*
minds

Your **mind** is the part of your brain that thinks, understands and remembers.
*I can't get that song out of my **mind**.*

mind *verb*
minds, minding, minded

If you **mind** something, it annoys you.
*It was hard work but she didn't **mind**.*

mine

Mine means belonging to me.
*That isn't your bag, it's **mine**.*

84

mine *noun*
mines

A **mine** is a deep hole or tunnel where people go to dig things like gold or diamonds out of rock.

minus

You use **minus** when you take one number away from another number.
*Three **minus** two is one.*

minute *noun*
minutes

A **minute** is used for measuring time. There are sixty seconds in one **minute**.
*The food will take 20 **minutes** to cook.*

minute *adjective*

Something that is **minute** is very small.
*You only need to use a **minute** amount of glue.*

miss *verb*
misses, missing, missed

1 If you **miss** something that you are trying to hit or catch, you do not manage to hit it or catch it.
*I jumped, but **missed** the ball.*

2 If you **miss** something, you do not notice it.
*What did he say? I **missed** it.*

3 If you **miss** someone who is not with you, you feel sad that they are not there.
*The boys **miss** their father.*

Miss

You use **Miss** in front of the name of a girl or a woman who is not married when you are talking to her or talking about her.
*Do you know **Miss** Smith?*

mistake *noun*
mistakes

A **mistake** is something that is not correct.
*I made three **mistakes** in my letter.*

mix *verb*
mixes, mixing, mixed

If you **mix** things, you put different things together to make something new.
***Mix** the sugar with the butter.*

mixture *noun*
mixtures

A **mixture** is what you make when you mix different things together.
*The drink is a **mixture** of orange and apple juice.*

mobile phone *noun*
mobile phones

A **mobile phone** is a small phone that you can take everywhere with you.

model *noun*
models

1 A **model** is a small copy of something.
*I made the **model** house with paper and glue.*

2 A **model** is a person whose job is to wear and show new clothes.
*The **model** in the picture was very tall.*

mole *noun*
moles

1 A **mole** is a natural dark spot on your skin.
*She has a **mole** on the side of her nose.*

2 A **mole** is a small animal with black fur that lives under the ground.

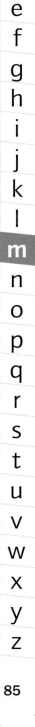

a
b
c
d
e
f
g
h
i
j
k
l
m
n
o
p
q
r
s
t
u
v
w
x
y
z

A
B
C
D
E
F
G
H
I
J
K
L
M
N
O
P
Q
R
S
T
U
V
W
X
Y
Z

moment *noun*
moments

A **moment** is a very short period of time.
*He stopped for a **moment**.*

Monday *noun*
Mondays

Monday is the day after Sunday and before Tuesday.
*I went back to school on **Monday**.*

money *noun*

Money is what you use to buy things.
*Cars cost a lot of **money**.*

monkey *noun*
monkeys

A **monkey** is an animal that has a long tail and can climb trees.

monster *noun*
monsters

In stories, a **monster** is a big, ugly creature that frightens people.
*The film is about a **monster** in the wardrobe.*

month *noun*
months

A **month** is one part of a year. There are twelve **months** in one year.
*We are going on holiday next **month**.*

moon *noun*
moons

The **moon** shines in the sky at night and moves around the earth every month.
*The first man on the **moon** was Neil Armstrong.*

more

You use **more** to talk about a greater amount of something.
*He has **more** chips than me.*

morning *noun*
mornings

The **morning** is the early part of the day, before lunch.
*What do you want to do tomorrow **morning**?*

most

1   **Most** of a group of things or people means nearly all of them.
    ***Most** of the houses here are very old.*

2   The **most** means the largest amount.
    *Who has the **most** money?*

moth *noun*
moths

A **moth** is an insect like a butterfly that usually flies at night.

mother *noun*
mothers

A **mother** is a woman who has a child.

motorbike *noun*
motorbikes

A **motorbike** is a large bike with an engine.

motorway *noun*
motorways

A **motorway** is a wide road for travelling long distances fast.

mountain *noun*
mountains

A **mountain** is a very high area of land with steep sides.
*Ben Nevis is the highest **mountain** in Scotland.*

mouse *noun*
mice

1 A **mouse** is a small animal with a long tail.

2 You use a **mouse** to move things on a computer screen.

mouth *noun*
mouths

Your **mouth** is the part of your face that you use for eating or talking.
*When you cough, please cover your **mouth**.*

move *verb*
moves, moving, moved

1 When you **move** something, you put it in a different place.
*The man asked her to **move** her car.*

2 If you **move**, you go to live in a different place.
*She's **moving** to London next month.*

Mr

You use **Mr** before a man's name when you are talking to him or talking about him.
*Our history teacher's name is **Mr** Jones.*

Mrs

You use **Mrs** before a married woman's name when you are talking to her or talking about her.
*How are you, **Mrs** Smith?*

Ms

You use **Ms** before a woman's name when you are talking to her or talking about her.
*The message is for **Ms** Clark.*

much

You use **much** to talk about a large amount of something.
*I ate too **much** food.*

mud *noun*

Mud is a mixture of earth and water.
*There was thick **mud** on my football boots.*

muddy *adjective*
muddier, muddiest

If something is **muddy**, it is covered with mud.
*My boots are all **muddy**!*

mug *noun*
mugs

A **mug** is a deep cup with straight sides.
*He poured tea into the **mugs**.*

a
b
c
d
e
f
g
h
i
j
k
l
m
n
o
p
q
r
s
t
u
v
w
x
y
z

87

A
B
C
D
E
F
G
H
I
J
K
L
M
N
O
P
Q
R
S
T
U
V
W
X
Y
Z

multiplication *noun*

Multiplication is when you multiply one number by another.

multiply *verb*
multiplies, multiplying, multiplied

If you **multiply** a number, you add it to itself a number of times.
*You get 24 if you **multiply** three by eight.*

mum or mummy *noun*
mums or **mummies**

Mum or **mummy** is a name for your mother.

muscle *noun*
muscles

Your **muscles** are the parts inside your body that help you move.
*Sport helps to keep your **muscles** strong.*

museum *noun*
museums

A **museum** is a building where you can look at interesting, old, and valuable things.
*Hundreds of people came to the **museum** to see the dinosaur bones.*

mushroom *noun*
mushrooms

A **mushroom** is a plant with a short stem and a round top that you can eat.
*There are many types of wild **mushroom**, and some of them are poisonous.*

music *noun*

Music is the sound that you make when you sing or play instruments.
*What's your favourite **music**?*

musical instrument *noun*
musical instruments

A **musical instrument** is an instrument that you use to play music, like a piano or a guitar.

must *verb*

You use **must** to show that you think something is very important.
*You **must** tell the police all the facts.*

mustn't

Mustn't is short for **must not**.
*I **mustn't** forget to take my key with me.*

my

You use **my** to show that something belongs to you.
*I went to sleep in **my** room.*

myself

You use **myself** when you are talking about yourself.
*I hurt **myself** when I fell down.*

mystery *noun*
mysteries

A **mystery** is something that you do not understand or know about.
*Why she's crying is a **mystery**.*

myth *noun*
myths

A **myth** is a very old story about magic, and strange people and creatures.

nail *noun*
nails

1   A **nail** is a thin piece of metal. It is flat at one end and it has a point at the other end.
    *A picture hung on a **nail** in the wall.*

2   Your **nails** are the thin hard parts that grow at the ends of your fingers and toes.
    *Try to keep your **nails** short.*

name *noun*
names

A person's **name** is the word or words that you use to talk to them, or to talk about them.
*Is your **name** Peter?*

narrow *adjective*
narrower, narrowest

Something that is **narrow** is a small distance from one side to the other.
*We walked through the town's **narrow** streets.*

nasty *adjective*
nastier, nastiest

Something that is **nasty** is horrible.
*That's a **nasty** thing to say!*

natural *adjective*

Natural things come from nature.
*The **natural** home of these animals is under the ground.*

nature *noun*

Nature is all the animals, plants, and other things in the world that people did not make or change.
*We watched **nature** all around us from our camp in the forest.*

naughty *adjective*
naughtier, naughtiest

A **naughty** child does things which are bad.
*She was so **naughty**, her mother sent her to bed early.*

near *adjective*
nearer, nearest

If something is **near** a place, thing, or person, it is not far away from them.
*We are very **near** my house.*

nearly

Nearly means almost.
*It's **nearly** five o'clock.*

neat *adjective*
neater, neatest

A **neat** place or person is clean and tidy.
*She made sure that her room was **neat** before she left.*

neck *noun*
necks

Your **neck** is the part of your body between your head and the rest of your body.
*He wore a gold chain around his **neck**.*

a b c d e f g h i j k l m n o p q r s t u v w x y z

A
B
C
D
E
F
G
H
I
J
K
L
M
N
O
P
Q
R
S
T
U
V
W
X
Y
Z

necklace *noun*
necklaces

A **necklace** is a chain of beads or jewels that you wear around your neck.
*She's wearing a beautiful **necklace**.*

need *verb*
needs, needing, needed

If you **need** something, you believe that you must have it or do it.
*I **need** some more money.*

needle *noun*
needles

A **needle** is a small, thin metal tool with a sharp point that you use for sewing.
*If you get me a **needle** and thread, I'll sew the button on.*

needn't

Needn't is short for **need not**.
*You **needn't** come with us if you don't want to.*

neighbour *noun*
neighbours

Your **neighbours** are the people who live around you.
*I met our **neighbour** when I went to the shops.*

nephew *noun*
nephews

Someone's **nephew** is the son of their sister or brother.
*I have a **nephew** who is still a baby.*

nervous *adjective*

If you are **nervous** about something, it worries you and you are rather afraid.
*I tried not to show that I was **nervous**.*

nest *noun*
nests

A **nest** is the place where a bird keeps its eggs or its babies.
*There were three small eggs in the bird's **nest**.*

net *noun*
nets

A **net** is made from pieces of string or rope tied together with holes between them. It is for catching things like fish, or the ball in some sports.
*The idea is to throw the ball into the top of the **net**.*

never

Never means at no time in the past, present or future.
***Never** look straight at the sun.*

new *adjective*
newer, newest

1 Something that is **new** was not there before.
  *They discovered a **new** medicine for his illness.*

2 If something is **new**, nobody has used it before.
  *I am wearing my **new** shoes.*

3 A **new** thing or person is a different one from the one you had before.
  *We have a **new** history teacher.*

news *noun*

News is information that you did not know before.
*We waited and waited for **news** of him.*

newspaper *noun*
newspapers

A **newspaper** is a number of large sheets of paper with news and other information printed on them.
*They read about it in the **newspaper**.*

next *adjective*

The **next** thing is the one that comes immediately after this one or after the last one.
*I got up early the **next** morning.*

nice *adjective*
nicer, nicest

If something is **nice**, you like it.
*They live in a really **nice** house.*

niece *noun*
nieces

Someone's **niece** is the daughter of their sister or brother.
*He bought a present for his **niece**.*

night *noun*
nights

The **night** is the time when it is dark outside, and most people sleep.
*It's eleven o'clock at **night** in Beijing.*

nightdress *noun*
nightdresses

A **nightdress** is a loose dress that a woman or girl can wear to sleep in.

nightmare *noun*
nightmares

A **nightmare** is a dream that frightens or worries you.
*She had a **nightmare** last night.*

nine *noun*

Nine is the number 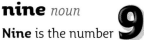.

no

You use **no** to say that something is not true or to refuse something.
*"Would you like a drink?"—"**No** thank you."*

nobody *noun*

Nobody means not one person.
*For a long time, **nobody** spoke.*

nod *verb*
nods, nodding, nodded

When you **nod**, you move your head up and down, usually to show that you agree.
*She **nodded** and smiled.*

noise *noun*
noises

A **noise** is a loud sound.
*Suddenly there was a **noise** like thunder.*

noisy *adjective*
noisier, noisiest

A **noisy** person or thing makes a lot of loud noise.
*It was a very **noisy** party.*

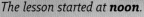

none

None means not one or not any.
***None** of us knew her.*

nonsense *noun*

If something is **nonsense**, it is not true or it is silly.
*My father said the story was **nonsense**.*

noon *noun*

Noon is twelve o'clock in the middle of the day.
*The lesson started at **noon**.*

a
b
c
d
e
f
g
h
i
j
k
l
m
n
o
p
q
r
s
t
u
v
w
x
y
z

A B C D E F G H I J K L M N O P Q R S T U V W X Y Z

north *noun*

The **north** is the direction to your left when you are looking towards the place where the sun rises.

nose *noun*
noses

Your **nose** is the part of your face above your mouth that you use for breathing and for noticing smells.
*She sneezed and blew her **nose**.*

nostril *noun*
nostrils

Your **nostrils** are the two holes at the end of your nose.
*Keeping your mouth closed, breathe in through your **nostrils**.*

note *noun*
notes

1 A **note** is a short letter or message.
*He wrote her a **note** and left it on the table.*

2 A **note** is one musical sound.
*She played some **notes** on her recorder.*

nothing

Nothing means not anything.
*There was **nothing** to do.*

notice *verb*
notices, noticing, noticed

If you **notice** something, you suddenly see or hear it.
*Did you **notice** him leave the room?*

notice *noun*
notices

A **notice** is a sign that gives information or instructions.
*The **notice** said "Please close the door".*

noun *noun*
nouns

A **noun** is a word that is used for talking about a person or thing. Examples of **nouns** are "child", "table", "sun", and "strength".

November *noun*

November is the month after October and before December. It has 30 days.

now

You use **now** to talk about the present time.
*I must go **now**.*

nowhere

Nowhere means not anywhere.
*There's **nowhere** quiet for me to do my homework.*

number *noun*
numbers

A **number** is a word that you use to count.
*What **number** is your house?*

nurse *noun*
nurses

A **nurse** is a person whose job is to care for people who are ill.
*She thanked the **nurses** at the hospital.*

nut *noun*
nuts

A **nut** is a dry fruit with a hard shell.
***Nuts** and seeds are very good for you.*

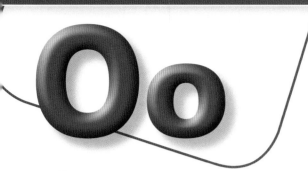

Oo

oak *noun*
oaks

An **oak** tree is a big, tall tree with a wide trunk. Its wood is good for making furniture.

oar *noun*
oars

An **oar** is a long piece of wood with a wide, flat end, used for moving a boat through the water.

obey *verb*
obeys, obeying, obeyed

If you **obey** a person or an order, you do what you are told to do.

ocean *noun*
oceans

An **ocean** is a big sea.
We crossed the Atlantic Ocean.

o'clock *noun*

You say **o'clock** when saying what time it is.
It is eight o'clock in the morning.

octagon *noun*
octagons

An **octagon** is a shape with eight straight sides.

October *noun*

October is the month after September and before November. It has 31 days.

octopus *noun*
octopuses

An **octopus** is a soft ocean animal with eight long arms.

odd *adjective*
odder, oddest

1 If something is **odd**, it is strange or unusual. *There was an odd smell in the kitchen.*

2 You say that two things are **odd** when they do not belong to the same set or pair. *I'm wearing odd socks.*

3 **Odd** numbers, such as 3 and 17, are numbers that cannot be divided by the number two.

off

1 If you take something **off** another thing, it is no longer on it. *He took his feet off the desk.*

2 When something that uses electricity is **off**, it is not using electricity. *The light was off.*

offer *verb*
offers, offering, offered

If you **offer** something to someone, you ask them if they would like to have it.
He offered his seat to the young woman.

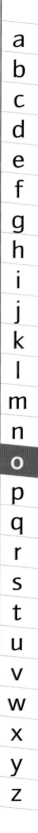

a
b
c
d
e
f
g
h
i
j
k
l
m
n
o
p
q
r
s
t
u
v
w
x
y
z

A
B
C
D
E
F
G
H
I
J
K
L
M
N
O
P
Q
R
S
T
U
V
W
X
Y
Z

office *noun*
offices

An **office** is a room where people work at desks.

often

Something that happens **often** happens many times or a lot of the time.

oil *noun*

Oil is a thick liquid.
We need some cooking oil.

old *adjective*
older, oldest

1 An **old** person is someone who has lived for a long time.
An old lady sat next to me.

2 An **old** thing is something that somebody made a long time ago.
We have a very old car.

on

1 If someone or something is **on** a surface, it is resting there.
There was a large box on the table.

2 When something that uses electricity is **on**, it is using electricity.
The television is on.

once

If something happens **once**, it happens one time only.
I met her once, at a party.

one *noun*

One is the number **1**.

onion *noun*
onions

An **onion** is a small, round vegetable with a brown skin like paper and a very strong taste.

only

1 If you talk about the **only** thing or person, you mean that there are no others.
It was the only shop in the town.

2 You use **only** when you are saying how small or short something is.
Their house is only a few miles from here.

3 If you are an **only** child, you have no brothers or sisters.

open *verb*
opens, opening, opened

1 When you **open** something, or when it **opens**, you move it so that it is no longer closed.
She opened the door.

2 When a shop or office **opens**, people are able to go in.
The banks will open again on Monday morning.

opposite

1 If one thing is **opposite** another, it is across from it.
Jennie sat opposite Sam at breakfast.

2 If things are **opposite**, they are as different as they can be.
We watched the cars driving in the opposite direction.

orange *noun/adjective*

1 An **orange** is a round fruit with a thick skin and lots of juice.

2 **Orange** is a colour between red and yellow.
Tigers are orange with black stripes.

orchestra *noun*
orchestras

An **orchestra** is a large group of people who play music together.
The orchestra began to play.

order *verb*

orders, ordering, ordered

If you **order** someone to do something, you tell them to do it.

*She **ordered** him to leave.*

ordinary *adjective*

Ordinary means not special or different in any way.

*It was just an **ordinary** day.*

other *adjective*

others

Other people or things are different people or things.

*All the **other** children had gone home.*

our

You use **our** to show that something belongs to you and one or more other people.

***Our** house is near the school.*

ours

You use **ours** when you are talking about something that belongs to you and one or more other people.

*That car is **ours**.*

out

1 If you go **out** of a place, you leave it.
   *She ran **out** of the house.*

2 If you are **out**, you are not at home.
   *I called you yesterday, but you were **out**.*

3 If a light is **out**, it is no longer shining.
   *All the lights were **out** in the house.*

outside

1 The **outside** of something is the part that covers the rest of it.
   *They are painting the **outside** of the building.*

2 If you are **outside**, you are not in a building.
   *Let's play **outside**.*

oval *adjective*

Oval things have a shape like an egg.

*She has an **oval** table.*

oven *noun*

ovens

An **oven** is the part of a cooker like a large metal box with a door.

over

1 If one thing is **over** another thing, the first thing is above or higher than the second thing.
   *There was a lamp **over** the table.*

2 If something is **over**, it has finished.
   *The class is **over**.*

owe *verb*

owes, owing, owed

If you **owe** money to someone, you have to pay money to them.

*He **owes** him $50.*

owl *noun*

owls

An **owl** is a bird with large eyes that hunts at night.

own

You use **own** to say that something belongs to you.

*Jennifer wanted her **own** room.*

ox *noun*

oxen

An **ox** is a kind of bull that is used for carrying or pulling things.

a
b
c
d
e
f
g
h
i
j
k
l
m
n
o
p
q
r
s
t
u
v
w
x
y
z

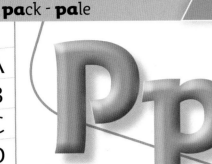

pack *verb*
packs, packing, packed

When you **pack** a bag, you put clothes and other things into it, because you are going away.

paddle *noun*
paddles

A **paddle** is a short oar. You use it to move a small boat through water.

paddle *verb*
paddles, paddling, paddled

1 If someone **paddles** a boat, they move it using a paddle.
2 If you **paddle**, you walk in shallow water.

page *noun*
pages

A **page** is one side of a piece of paper in a book, a magazine, or a newspaper.
Turn to page 4.

paid

⇨ Look at **pay**.
Daddy paid for the sweets.

pain *noun*
pains

Pain is the feeling that you have in a part of your body, because of illness or an accident.
I felt a sudden sharp pain in my ankle.

painful *adjective*

If a part of your body is **painful**, it hurts.
His right knee is very painful.

paint *noun*
paints

Paint is a liquid used to decorate buildings, or to make a picture.
Can I use some of your red paint?

paint *verb*
paints, painting, painted

1 If you **paint** something on a piece of paper or cloth, you make a picture of it using paint.
He likes painting flowers.
2 If you **paint** a wall or a door, you cover it with paint.

painting *noun*
paintings

A **painting** is a picture made with paint.
He's doing a painting of a bowl of fruit.

pair *noun*
pairs

A **pair** of things is two things of the same size and shape that are used together.
She wore a pair of plain black shoes.

palace *noun*
palaces

A **palace** is a very large house where important people live.

pale *adjective*
paler, palest

A **pale** colour is not strong or bright.
She's wearing a pale blue dress.

palm *noun*
palms

1 A **palm** or a **palm tree** is a tree that grows in hot countries. It has long leaves at the top, and no branches.

2 The **palm** of your hand is the inside part of your hand, between your fingers and your wrist.

panda *noun*
pandas

A **panda** is a large animal with black and white fur.

pantomime *noun*
pantomimes

A **pantomime** is a play that has a funny story with music and songs.

paper *noun*
papers

1 **Paper** is a material that you write on or wrap things with.
*He wrote his name down on a piece of **paper**.*

2 A **paper** is a newspaper.

parcel *noun*
parcels

A **parcel** is something that is wrapped in paper.

parent *noun*
parents

Your **parents** are your mother and father.

park *noun*
parks

A **park** is a place with grass and trees. People go to **parks** to take exercise or play games.

park *verb*
parks, parking, parked

When someone **parks** a car, they leave it somewhere.
*They **parked** in the street outside the house.*

parrot *noun*
parrots

A **parrot** is a bird with a curved beak and bright feathers.
Parrots' feet have two toes at the front and two at the back.

part *noun*
parts

Part of something is a piece of it.

party *noun*
parties

A **party** is a time when people meet to have fun.
*She's having a birthday **party**.*

pass *verb*
passes, passing, passed

1 When you **pass** someone, you go by them.
*We **passed** them on our way here.*

2 If you **pass** something to someone, you give it to them.
*He **passed** a note to his friend.*

3 If you **pass** a test, you do well.

passenger *noun*
passengers

A **passenger** is a person who is travelling in a vehicle, but who is not driving.

a
b
c
d
e
f
g
h
i
j
k
l
m
n
o
p
q
r
s
t
u
v
w
x
y
z

A
B
C
D
E
F
G
H
I
J
K
L
M
N
O
P
Q
R
S
T
U
V
W
X
Y
Z

past *noun*

The **past** is the period of time before now.
*In the **past**, there weren't any computers.*

past

1 Something that is **past** a place is on the other side of it.
*It's just **past** the school there.*

2 You use **past** when you are telling the time.
*It was ten **past** eleven.*

pasta *noun*

Pasta is a mixture of flour, eggs, and water.
***Pasta** comes in lots of shapes, even letters of the alphabet.*

paste *verb*
pastes, pasting, pasted

1 If you **paste** something on to a surface, you stick it with glue.

2 If you **paste** words or pictures on a computer, you copy them from one place and put them somewhere new.
*You can **paste** by holding down the Ctrl key and pressing V.*

pastry *noun*

Pastry is a mixture of flour, butter, and water. People make it flat and thin so that they can use it to make pies.

path *noun*
paths

A **path** is a strip of ground that people walk along.
*We followed the **path** along the cliff.*

patient *adjective*

If you are **patient**, you don't get angry quickly.

patient *noun*
patients

A **patient** is someone that a nurse or a doctor is looking after.

pattern *noun*
patterns

A **pattern** is a group of repeated shapes.
*The carpet had a **pattern** of light and dark stripes.*

paw *noun*
paws

The **paws** of an animal such as a cat, dog, or bear are its feet.
*The kitten was black with white **paws**.*

pay *verb*
pays, paying, paid

If you **pay** for something, you give someone an amount of money for it.
*Did you **pay** for those sweets?*

peach *noun*
peaches

A **peach** is a round fruit with a soft red and orange skin.

peanut *noun*
peanuts

Peanuts are small nuts that you can eat.

pear *noun*
pears

A **pear** is a fruit which is narrow at the top and wide and round at the bottom.

peas *noun*

Peas are small, round, green vegetables.

pebble *noun*
pebbles

A **pebble** is a small, smooth stone.

pedal *noun*
pedals

The **pedals** on a bicycle are the two parts that you push with your feet to make the bicycle move.

peel *noun*

The **peel** of a fruit is its skin.

peg *noun*
pegs

A **peg** is a small piece of metal or wood on a wall that you hang things on.

pen *noun*
pens

A **pen** is a long thin tool that you use for writing with ink.

pencil *noun*
pencils

A **pencil** is a thin piece of wood with a black material through the middle that you use to write or draw with.

penguin *noun*
penguins

A **penguin** is a black and white bird that lives in very cold places. **Penguins** can swim but they cannot fly.

pentagon *noun*
pentagons

A **pentagon** is a shape with five straight sides.

people *noun*

People are men, women, and children. *Lots of **people** came to the party.*

pepper *noun*
peppers

1 **Pepper** is a powder with a hot taste that you put on food.

2 A **pepper** is a green, red, or yellow vegetable with seeds inside it.

period *noun*
periods

A **period** is a length of time.

person *noun*
people

A **person** is a man, a woman, or a child.

pest *noun*
pests

Pests are insects or small animals that damage crops or food.

pet *noun*
pets

A **pet** is a tame animal that you keep in your home.

a
b
c
d
e
f
g
h
i
j
k
l
m
n
o
p
q
r
s
t
u
v
w
x
y
z

A
B
C
D
E
F
G
H
I
J
K
L
M
N
O
P
Q
R
S
T
U
V
W
X
Y
Z

petal *noun*
petals

The **petals** of a flower are the thin parts on the outside that are a bright colour.

phone *noun*
phones

A **phone** is a piece of equipment that you use to talk to someone in another place.
*Two minutes later the **phone** rang.*

photograph *noun*
photographs

A **photograph** is a picture that you take with a camera.
*She took lots of **photographs** of her friends.*

piano *noun*
pianos

A **piano** is a large instrument for playing music. You play it by pressing the black and white keys.

pick *verb*
picks, picking, picked

1 If you **pick** someone, you choose them.
2 When you **pick** flowers, fruit, or leaves, you take them from a plant or tree.
   *I've **picked** some flowers from the garden.*

picnic *noun*
picnics

When people have a **picnic**, they eat a meal outside, usually in a park or a forest, or at the beach.
*We're going on a **picnic** tomorrow.*

picture *noun*
pictures

A **picture** is a drawing or painting.

pie *noun*
pies

A **pie** is a dish of fruit, meat, or vegetables that is covered with pastry and baked.
*We each had a slice of apple **pie**.*

piece *noun*
pieces

A **piece** of something is a part of it.
*You must only take one **piece** of cake.*

pig *noun*
pigs

A **pig** is a farm animal with a fat body and short legs.

pigeon *noun*
pigeons

A **pigeon** is a large grey bird.

pile *noun*
piles

A **pile** of things is several of them lying on top of each other.
*We searched through the **pile** of boxes.*

pill *noun*
pills

Pills are small solid round pieces of medicine that you swallow.

pillow noun
pillows

A **pillow** is something soft that you rest your head on when you are in bed.

pilot noun
pilots

A **pilot** is a person who controls an aircraft.

pin noun
pins

A **pin** is a very small thin piece of metal with a point at one end.

pineapple noun
pineapples

A **pineapple** is a large sweet yellow fruit with a lot of juice. Its skin is brown, thick, and very rough.

pipe noun
pipes

A **pipe** is a long tube that water or gas can flow through.
*They are going to take out the old water **pipes**.*

pirate noun
pirates

Pirates are people who attack ships and steal things from them.
*They have to find the **pirates** and the hidden gold.*

pizza noun
pizzas

A **pizza** is a flat, round piece of bread. **Pizzas** are covered with cheese and tomatoes.
*Bake the **pizza** in a hot oven.*

place noun
places

1 A **place** is a building, area, town, or country.
   *This is the **place** where I was born.*

2 A **place** is also where something belongs.
   *He put the picture back in its **place** on the shelf.*

plain adjective
plainer, plainest

Something that is **plain** is ordinary and not special.

plan noun
plans

A **plan** is a way of doing something that you work out before you do it.
*I've got a **plan** for getting out of here.*

plane noun
planes

A **plane** is a large vehicle with wings and engines that flies through the air.

planet noun
planets

You find **planets** in space. They move around stars. The Earth is a **planet**.

a
b
c
d
e
f
g
h
i
j
k
l
m
n
o
p
q
r
s
t
u
v
w
x
y
z

101

A
B
C
D
E
F
G
H
I
J
K
L
M
N
O
P
Q
R
S
T
U
V
W
X
Y
Z

plant *noun*
plants

A **plant** is a living thing that grows in the earth. **Plants** have a stem, leaves, and roots.

plaster *noun*
plasters

1 A **plaster** is a strip of material with a soft part in the middle. You can cover a cut on your body with a **plaster**.

2 **Plaster** is a paste which people put on walls and ceilings so that they are smooth.
*There were huge cracks in the **plaster**.*

plastic *noun*

Plastic is a material that is light but strong. It is made in factories.
*He put his sweets in a **plastic** bag.*

plate *noun*
plates

A **plate** is a flat dish that is used for holding food.
*She pushed her **plate** away.*

platform *noun*
platforms

A **platform** in a station is the place where you wait for a train.

play *verb*
plays, playing, played

1 When you **play**, you spend time using toys and taking part in games.
*She was **playing** with her dolls.*

2 If you **play** an instrument, you make music with it.

playground *noun*
playgrounds

A **playground** is a special area where children can play.

please

You say **please** when you are asking someone to do something.
*Can you help us, **please**?*

plenty *noun*

If there is **plenty** of something, there is a lot of it.
*Don't worry. There's still **plenty** of time.*

plough *noun*
ploughs

A **plough** is a large tool that is used on a farm. Farmers pull it across a field to make the earth loose, so that they can plant seeds.

plus

You say **plus** to show that you are adding one number to another.
*Two **plus** two is four.*

pocket *noun*
pockets

A **pocket** is a small bag that is part of your clothes.
*He put the key in his **pocket**.*

poem *noun*
poems

A **poem** is a piece of writing. When people write a **poem**, they choose the words in a very careful way, so that they sound beautiful.

point *noun*
points

1 The **point** of something is its thin, sharp end. Needles and knives have **points**.
2 A **point** is a mark that you win in a game or a sport.

point *verb*
points, pointing, pointed

If you **point** at something, you stick out your finger to show where it is.
*I **pointed** at the boy sitting near me.*

poisonous *adjective*

Something that is **poisonous** will kill you or hurt you if you swallow or touch it.

polar bear *noun*
polar bears

A **polar bear** is a large white bear which lives in the area around the North Pole.

police *noun*

The **police** are the people who make sure that people obey the law.

polite *adjective*

Someone who is **polite** behaves well.

pond *noun*
ponds

A **pond** is a small area of water.
*We can feed the ducks on the **pond**.*

pony *noun*
ponies

A **pony** is a small horse.

poor *adjective*
poorer, poorest

Someone who is **poor** doesn't have much money and doesn't own many things.

possible *adjective*

If something is **possible** it can happen.

post *verb*
posts, posting, posted

If you **post** a letter, you put a stamp on it and send it to someone.

poster *noun*
posters

A **poster** is a large notice or picture that you stick on a wall.

potato *noun*
potatoes

Potatoes are hard round white vegetables with brown or red skins. They grow under the ground.

a
b
c
d
e
f
g
h
i
j
k
l
m
n
o
p
q
r
s
t
u
v
w
x
y
z

A
B
C
D
E
F
G
H
I
J
K
L
M
N
O
P
Q
R
S
T
U
V
W
X
Y
Z

pour *verb*
pours, pouring, poured

If you **pour** something like water, you make it flow out of a container.

powder *noun*

Powder is a fine dry dust, like flour.

power *noun*

1 If someone has **power**, they have control over people.
*He has the **power** to keep you in after school.*

2 The **power** of something is its strength.
*The engine doesn't often work at full **power**.*

practise *verb*
practises, practising, practised

If you **practise** something, you do it often in order to do it better.
*I've been **practising** my song.*

present *noun*
presents

1 The **present** is the period of time that is taking place now.

2 A **present** is something that you give to someone for them to keep.
*She got a **present** for her birthday.*

present *adjective*

If someone is **present** somewhere, they are there.
*He wasn't **present** when they called out his name.*

press *verb*
presses, pressing, pressed

If you **press** something, you push it hard.
***Press** the blue button.*

pretend *verb*
pretends, pretending, pretended

When you **pretend**, you act as if something is true, when you know it isn't.
*She **pretended** to be the teacher.*

pretty *adjective*
prettier, prettiest

If something is **pretty**, it is nice to look at.
*She was wearing a **pretty** necklace.*

price *noun*
prices

The **price** of something is how much you have to pay to buy it.
*Could you tell me the **price** of this car, please?*

prick *verb*
pricks, pricking, pricked

If you **prick** something, you stick something sharp like a pin or a knife into it.
*She **pricked** her finger on a pin.*

prince *noun*
princes

A **prince** is a boy or a man in the family of a king or queen.

princess *noun*
princesses

A **princess** is a girl or a woman in the family of a king or queen.

print *verb*
prints, printing, printed

1 If you **print** something, you use a machine to put words or pictures on paper.
2 If you **print** when you are writing, you do not join the letters together.

prison *noun*
prisons

A **prison** is a building where people who have broken the law are kept as a punishment.
*He was sent to **prison** for five years.*

prize *noun*
prizes

A **prize** is money or a special thing that you give to the person who wins a game, a race, or a competition.
*He won first **prize**.*

problem *noun*
problems

A **problem** is something or someone that makes thing difficult, or that makes you worry.

program *noun*
programs

A **program** is a set of instructions that a computer uses to do a job.

programme *noun*
programmes

A **programme** is a television or radio show.
*She is watching her favourite television **programme**.*

project *noun*
projects

A **project** is a plan that takes a lot of time and effort.
*It was a large building **project**.*

promise *verb*
promises, promising, promised

If you **promise** to do something, you say that you will be sure to do it.
*I **promise** that I'll help you all I can.*

pronoun *noun*
pronouns

A **pronoun** is a word that you use in place of a noun when you are talking about someone or something. "It" and "she" are **pronouns**.

proper *adjective*

The **proper** thing or way is the one that is right.
*Put things in their **proper** place.*

protect *verb*
protects, protecting, protected

If you **protect** something, you keep it safe.
*Make sure you **protect** your skin from the sun.*

proud *adjective*
prouder, proudest

If you feel **proud**, you feel pleased about something good that you or other people close to you have done.
*I was **proud** of our team today.*

pudding *noun*
puddings

A **pudding** is something sweet that you eat after your main meal.
*We had a delicious chocolate **pudding**.*

a
b
c
d
e
f
g
h
i
j
k
l
m
n
o
p
q
r
s
t
u
v
w
x
y
z

A
B
C
D
E
F
G
H
I
J
K
L
M
N
O
P
Q
R
S
T
U
V
W
X
Y
Z

puddle *noun*
puddles

A **puddle** is a small amount of water on the ground.
*Splashing in **puddles** is lots of fun.*

pull *verb*
pulls, pulling, pulled

When you **pull** something, you hold it and move it towards you.
*The dentist had to **pull** out all his teeth.*

punishment *noun*
punishments

Punishment is something done to someone because they have done something wrong.
*His father sent him to bed early as a **punishment** for being rude.*

pupil *noun*
pupils

The **pupils** at a school are the children who go there.
*Around 200 **pupils** go to this school.*

puppet *noun*
puppets

A **puppet** is a small model of a person or animal that you can move.

puppy *noun*
puppies

A **puppy** is a young dog.

purple *noun/adjective*

Purple is a mixture of red and blue.
*Some grapes are **purple**.*

purse *noun*
purses

A **purse** is a small bag that women use to carry money and other things.
*She reached in her **purse** for her money.*

push *verb*
pushes, pushing, pushed

When you **push** something, you press it in order to move it away from you.
*I **pushed** back my chair and stood up.*

put *verb*
puts, putting, put

When you **put** something somewhere, you move it there.
*He **put** the book on the desk.*

puzzle *verb*
puzzles, puzzling, puzzled

If something **puzzles** you, you do not understand it and you feel confused.
*There was something about her that **puzzled** me.*

pyjamas *noun*

Pyjamas are loose trousers and a jacket that you wear in bed.

pyramid *noun*
pyramids

A **pyramid** is a solid shape with a flat base and flat sides that make a point where they meet at the top.

quack *verb*
quacks, quacking, quacked

When a duck **quacks**, it makes a loud sound.
There were ducks quacking on the lawn.

quarrel *noun*
quarrels

A **quarrel** is an angry argument between people.
I had an awful quarrel with my brothers.

quarter *noun*
quarters

A **quarter** is one of four equal parts of something.
My sister ate a quarter of the chocolate cake.

queen *noun*
queens

A **queen** is a woman who rules a country, or a woman who is married to a king.
The crowd cheered when the queen went past.

question *noun*
questions

A **question** is something that you say or write to ask a person about something.
They asked her a lot of questions about her holiday.

queue *noun*
queues

A **queue** is a line of people or cars waiting for something.
He stood in the lunch queue for ten minutes.

quick *adjective*
quicker, quickest

Something that is **quick** moves or does things with great speed.
The cat was so quick that I couldn't catch it.

quickly

If you move or do something **quickly** you do it with great speed.
The girl ran quickly along the street.

quiet *adjective*
quieter, quietest

Someone who is **quiet** makes only a small amount of noise or no noise at all.
The baby was so quiet I didn't know he was there.

quite

Quite means a bit but not a lot.
I quite like her but she's not my best friend.

quiz *noun*
quizzes

A **quiz** is a game in which someone asks you questions to find out what you know.
After dinner we had a TV quiz and our team won.

a b c d e f g h i j k l m n o p **q** r s t u v w x y z

A
B
C
D
E
F
G
H
I
J
K
L
M
N
O
P
Q
R
S
T
U
V
W
X
Y
Z

rabbit *noun*
rabbits

A **rabbit** is a small animal with long ears. **Rabbits** live in holes in the ground.
*The children were excited when they heard they were getting a pet **rabbit**.*

race *noun*
races

A **race** is a competition to see who is fastest, for example in running or driving.
*Nobody can beat my sister in a **race**.*

radiator *noun*
radiators

A **radiator** is a metal thing filled with hot water or steam. **Radiators** keep rooms warm.
*I burned myself on the **radiator** in the bathroom.*

radio *noun*
radios

A **radio** is a piece of equipment you use to hear programmes with talking, news and music.
*Turn on the **radio** for the news please.*

railway *noun*
railways

A **railway** is a special road for trains, with stations along it. **Railways** have two metal lines that are always the same distance apart.
*The house was beside the **railway**.*

rain *noun*

Rain is water that falls from the clouds in small drops.
*My mother told me not to go out in the **rain**.*

rainbow *noun*
rainbows

A **rainbow** is a half circle of different colours in the sky. You can sometimes see a **rainbow** when it rains.
*A **rainbow** appeared when the storm was over.*

ran

➡ Look at **run**.
*I **ran** to school because I was late.*

rang

➡ Look at **ring**.
*I got worried when the phone **rang**.*

rare *adjective*
rarer, rarest

Something that is **rare** is not seen or heard very often.
*We are lucky to see this bird because it is very **rare**.*

raspberry *noun*
raspberries

A **raspberry** is a small soft red fruit. **Raspberries** grow on bushes.
*Would you like some **raspberries** with your ice cream?*

rat *noun*
rats

A **rat** is an animal that looks like a mouse. A **rat** has a long tail and sharp teeth.
*The old house was full of **rats**.*

rather

You use **rather** to mean "a little bit".
*I thought the party was **rather** boring.*

raw *adjective*

Raw food has not been cooked.
*There is a bowl of **raw** carrots and cauliflower on the table.*

reach *verb*
reaches, reaching, reached

1 When you **reach** a place, you arrive there.
*We will not **reach** home until midnight.*

2 If you **reach** somewhere, you move your arm and hand to take or touch something.
*I **reached** into my bag and brought out a pen.*

read *verb*
reads, reading, read

When you **read**, you look at written words and understand them, and sometimes say them aloud.
*My father **reads** me a story every night before I go to sleep.*

ready *adjective*

If you are **ready**, you are able to do something or go somewhere right now.
*It takes her a long time to get **ready** for school.*

real *adjective*

1 Something that is **real** is true and is not imagined.
*No, it wasn't a dream. It was **real**.*

2 If something is **real**, it is not a copy.
*Is your necklace **real** gold?*

really

1 You say **really** to show how much you mean something.
*I'm **really** sorry I can't come to your party.*

2 You say **really** to show that what you are saying is true.
*Are we **really** going to the zoo?*

reason *noun*
reasons

The **reason** for something is the fact which explains why it happens.
*You must have a good **reason** for being so late.*

receive *verb*
receives, receiving, received

When you **receive** something, someone gives it to you, or you get it after it has been sent to you.
*Did you **receive** the birthday card I sent you?*

recipe *noun*
recipes

A **recipe** is a list of food and a set of instructions telling you how to cook something.
*Do you have a **recipe** for chocolate cake?*

recite *verb*
recites, reciting, recited

When someone **recites** a poem or other piece of writing, they say it aloud after they have learned it.
*We each had to **recite** a poem in front of the class.*

record *noun*
records

A **record** is the best result ever.
*What's the world **record** for the 100 metres?*

record *verb*
records, recording, recorded

If you **record** something like a TV programme, you make a copy of it so that you can watch it later.
*Can you **record** the football for me please?*

recorder *noun*
recorders

A **recorder** is a small instrument in the shape of a pipe. You play a **recorder** by blowing into it and putting your fingers over the holes in it.
*He has been learning the **recorder** for three years.*

a
b
c
d
e
f
g
h
i
j
k
l
m
n
o
p
q
r
s
t
u
v
w
x
y
z

rectangle *noun*
rectangles

A **rectangle** is a shape with four straight sides.

red *noun/adjective*

Red is the colour of blood or a strawberry.
*Her dress is bright **red**.*

reflection *noun*
reflections

A **reflection** is something
you can see on a smooth,
shiny surface. What you see
is really in a different place.
***Reflections** always show things
the wrong way round.*

refuse *verb*
refuses, refusing, refused

If you **refuse** to do something, you say that
you will not do it.
*He **refuses** to have a bath.*

remember *verb*
**remembers, remembering,
remembered**

If you **remember** people or things from the
past, you can bring them into your mind and
think about them.
*I **remember** the first time I met him.*

remind *verb*
reminds, reminding, reminded

If someone **reminds** you about something,
they help you to remember it.
***Remind** me to buy a bottle of milk, will you?*

remove *verb*
removes, removing, removed

If you **remove** something from a place, you
take it away.
*When the cake is cooked, **remove** it from the oven.*

repair *verb*
**repairs, repairing,
repaired**

If you **repair** something
that is damaged or broken,
you fix it so that it works again.
*The man managed to
repair the broken tap.*

repeat *verb*
repeats, repeating, repeated

If you **repeat** something, you say it, write it,
or do it again.
*Please can you **repeat** the question?*

reply *verb*
replies, replying, replied

If you **reply** to something, you say or write
an answer.
*Will you please **reply** when I ask you a question.*

reptile *noun*
reptiles

A **reptile** is an animal
that has cold blood, rough
skin, and lays eggs. Snakes and
lizards are **reptiles**.

rescue *verb*
rescues, rescuing, rescued

If you **rescue** someone, you help them get
away from a dangerous place.
*The police **rescued** 20 people from the roof of
the building.*

rest *verb*
rests, resting, rested

If you **rest**, you sit or lie
down and do not do anything
active for a while.
*My grandmother always
rests in the afternoon.*

A B C D E F G H I J K L M N O P Q R S T U V W X Y Z

rest *noun*

The **rest** is the parts of something that are left.
*Who ate the **rest** of the cake?*

restaurant *noun*
restaurants

A **restaurant** is a place where you can buy and eat a meal.
*We had lunch in an Italian **restaurant**.*

result *noun*
results

A **result** is something that happens because another thing has happened.
*I got measles and as a **result** was off school for two weeks.*

return *verb*
returns, returning, returned

1 When you **return** to a place, you go back to it after you have been away.
*He **returned** to Japan after his holiday in England.*

2 If you **return** something to someone, you give it back to them.
*I forgot to **return** my library books.*

reward *noun*
rewards

A **reward** is something that is given to a person because they have done something good.
*The school gives **rewards** to children who behave well.*

rhinoceros *noun*
rhinoceroses

A **rhinoceros** is a large wild animal with thick grey skin.
A **rhinoceros** has one or two horns on its nose.

rhyme *verb*
rhymes, rhyming, rhymed

If two words **rhyme**, they have the same sound at the end of them.
*Sally **rhymes** with valley.*

rhythm *noun*
rhythms

Rhythm is something which is repeated again and again in the same way.
*Listen to the **rhythm** of the music.*

rib *noun*
ribs

Your **ribs** are the 12 pairs of curved bones that go round your body.
*He fell off his bike and broke a **rib**.*

ribbon *noun*
ribbons

A **ribbon** is a long narrow piece of cloth. You use **ribbons** to decorate things or tie them together.
*The girl's hair was tied with a blue and white **ribbon**.*

rice *noun*

Rice is white or brown grains from a plant. **Rice** grows in wet areas.
*The meal was chicken, **rice**, and vegetables.*

rich *adjective*
richer, richest

Someone who is **rich** has a lot of money and expensive things.
*She is a **rich** woman who owns a very large house.*

riddle *noun*
riddles

A **riddle** is a question that seems to be nonsense, but that has a clever answer.
*He asked the **riddle**, "What key cannot open a door?" and I answered, "a monkey".*

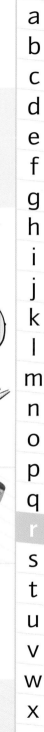

a
b
c
d
e
f
g
h
i
j
k
l
m
n
o
p
q
r
s
t
u
v
w
x
y
z

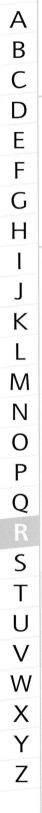

A
B
C
D
E
F
G
H
I
J
K
L
M
N
O
P
Q
R
S
T
U
V
W
X
Y
Z

ride *verb*

rides, riding, rode, ridden

When you **ride** a horse or a bike, you sit on it and control it as it moves along.
*The girl **rode** her horse along the beach.*

right *adjective*

1 If something is **right**, it is correct and there have been no mistakes.
*Only one child in the class knew the **right** answer to the teacher's question.*

2 The **right** side is the side that is towards the east when you look north.
*Most people write with their **right** hand.*

ring *verb*

rings, ringing, rang, rung

When a bell **rings**, it makes a clear, loud sound.
*The school bell **rings** at nine o'clock.*

ring *noun*

rings

A **ring** is a round piece of metal that you wear on a finger.
*He turned the **ring** on his finger.*

ripe *adjective*

riper, ripest

When fruit or grain is **ripe**, it is ready to be eaten.
*Don't eat the apples until they are **ripe**.*

rise *verb*

rises, rising, rose, risen

If something **rises**, it moves up.
*We watched the balloon **rise** into the sky.*

river *noun*

rivers

A **river** is a long line of water that flows into the sea.
*The Nile is one of the longest **rivers** in the world.*

road *noun*

roads

A **road** is a long piece of hard ground for vehicles to travel on.
*You must look both ways before you cross the **road**.*

roar *verb*

roars, roaring, roared

If a person, an animal or a thing **roars**, they make a very loud noise.
*The engines **roared** and the aeroplane started to move.*

robot *noun*

robots

A **robot** is a machine that can move and do things that it has been told to do.
*We have **robots** that we could send to the moon.*

rock *noun*

rocks

1 **Rock** is the hard material that is in the ground and in mountains.
*We tried to dig, but the ground was solid **rock**.*

2 A **rock** is a piece of this material.
*She picked up a **rock** and threw it into the lake.*

rock *verb*

rocks, rocking, rocked

If something **rocks**, it moves from side to side.

rocket *noun*

rockets

A **rocket** is a vehicle that people use to travel into space.
*This is the **rocket** that took them to the moon.*

rode

⇨ Look at **ride**.
*The man **rode** his bike down the hill.*

roll *verb*
rolls, rolling, rolled

When something **rolls**, it moves along a surface, turning over and over.
*The ball bounced out of the garden and **rolled** across the road.*

roof *noun*
roofs

The **roof** of a building is the bit on top that covers it.
*Our house is the one with the red **roof**.*

room *noun*
rooms

1 A **room** is a part of a building that has its own walls.
*A minute later he left the **room**.*

2 If there is **room** somewhere, there is a enough empty space.
*There isn't **room** for any more furniture in here.*

root *noun*
roots

The **roots** of a plant are the parts of it that grow under the ground.
*She dug a hole near the **roots** of an apple tree.*

rope *noun*
ropes

A **rope** is a type of very thick string that is made by twisting together several strings or wires.
*He tied the **rope** around his waist.*

rose *noun*
roses

A **rose** is a large garden flower with a lovely smell. **Roses** grow on bushes.
*The teacher was given a bunch of red **roses**.*

rough *adjective*
rougher, roughest

1 If something is **rough**, it is not smooth or even.
*His hands were **rough**.*

2 If you are **rough**, you are not being careful or gentle.
*Don't be so **rough** or you'll break it.*

round *adjective*
rounder, roundest

Something **round** is in the shape of a ball or a circle.
*There was a **round** table in the middle of the room.*

row *noun*
rows

A **row** is a line of things or people.
*Our house is opposite a **row** of shops.*

rub *verb*
rubs, rubbing, rubbed

If you **rub** something, you move your hand or a cloth backwards and forwards over it.
*I **rubbed** the window and looked outside.*

rubber *noun*
rubbers

1 **Rubber** is a strong material that stretches. **Rubber** is used to make things like tyres and boots for wet weather.

2 A **rubber** is a small piece of rubber used to remove pencil mistakes.
*Have you got a **rubber** in your pencil case?*

a b c d e f g h i j k l m n o p q r s t u v w x y z

113

A
B
C
D
E
F
G
H
I
J
K
L
M
N
O
P
Q
R
S
T
U
V
W
X
Y
Z

rubbish *noun*

Rubbish is things like empty packs and used paper that you throw away.

rude *adjective*
ruder, rudest

If people are **rude**, they are not polite.
*It is **rude** to ask for something without saying "please".*

ruin *verb*
ruins, ruining, ruined

If you **ruin** something, you destroy or spoil it.
*The rain **ruined** the party.*

rule *noun*
rules

Rules are instructions that tell you what you must do or must not do.
*Can you explain the **rules** of cricket to me?*

rule *verb*
rules, ruling, ruled

Someone who **rules** a country controls it.

ruler *noun*
rulers

1 A **ruler** is a long, flat piece of wood or plastic with straight edges. You use a **ruler** for measuring things or drawing straight lines.
2 A **ruler** is also a person who rules a country.
*He was **ruler** of France at that time.*

run *verb*
runs, running, ran, run

When you **run**, you move very quickly on your legs.
*It's very dangerous to **run** across the road.*

rung

⇨ Look at **ring**.
*They had **rung** the door bell when I was in the shower.*

sad *adjective*
sadder, saddest

If you are **sad**, you don't feel happy.
*I'm **sad** that he is leaving.*

safe *adjective*
safer, safest

If you are **safe**, you are not in any danger.
*Is it **safe**?*

said

⇨ Look at **say**.
*That is what she **said** to me.*

sail *noun*
sails

Sails are large pieces of cloth on a boat that catch the wind and move the boat along.

salad *noun*
salads

A **salad** is a mixture of vegetables and sometimes other foods. You usually eat **salads** cold.

salt *noun*

Salt is a white powder that you use to make food taste better.
*Now add **salt** and pepper.*

same *adjective*

If two things are the **same**, they are like one another.

*The two cats look the **same**.*

sand *noun*

Sand is a powder made of very small pieces of stone. Deserts and most beaches are made of **sand**.

sandal *noun*
sandals

Sandals are light shoes that you wear in warm weather.

*He put on a pair of old **sandals**.*

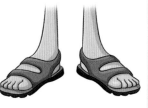

sandwich *noun*
sandwiches

A **sandwich** is two slices of bread with another food such as cheese or meat between them.

*She ate a large **sandwich**.*

sang

⇨ Look at **sing**.
*She **sang** a happy song.*

sank

⇨ Look at **sink**.
*The boat **sank** in the storm.*

sari *noun*
saris

A **sari** is a long piece of material worn folded around the body by women.

*She was wearing a new yellow **sari**.*

sat

⇨ Look at **sit**.
*She **sat** down next to the fire.*

satellite *noun*
satellites

A **satellite** is a machine that is sent into space to receive and send back information.

Saturday *noun*
Saturdays

Saturday is the day after Friday and before Sunday.

*He called her on **Saturday** morning.*

saucepan *noun*
saucepans

A **saucepan** is a deep metal container with a long handle and a lid. **Saucepans** are used for cooking.

*Put the potatoes in a **saucepan** and boil them.*

saucer *noun*
saucers

A **saucer** is a small curved plate that you put under a cup.

a b c d e f g h i j k l m n o p q r **s** t u v w x y z

115

A
B
C
D
E
F
G
H
I
J
K
L
M
N
O
P
Q
R
S
T
U
V
W
X
Y
Z

sausage *noun*
sausages

A **sausage** is a mixture of very small pieces of meat and other foods, inside a long thin skin.

save *verb*
saves, saving, saved

1 If you **save** someone or something, you help them to escape from danger.
*He **saved** the boy from drowning.*

2 If you **save** something, you keep it because you will need it later.
*She was **saving** her money.*

saw

⇨ Look at **see**.
*We **saw** her walking down the street.*

saw *noun*
saws

A **saw** is a metal tool for cutting wood.
*He used a **saw** to cut the branches off the tree.*

say *verb*
says, saying, said

When you **say** something, you talk.
*She **said** that they were very pleased.*

scale *noun*
scales

Scales are small, flat pieces of hard skin that cover the body of animals like fish and snakes.

scales *noun*

Scales are a machine used for weighing things.
*He weighed flour on the **scales**.*

scared *adjective*

If you are **scared** of something it frightens you.
*She is **scared** of spiders.*

school *noun*
schools

A **school** is a place where people go to learn.
*The **school** was built in the 1960s.*

science *noun*
sciences

Science is the study of natural things.

scissors *noun*

Scissors are a small tool for cutting with two sharp parts that are joined together.
*Cut the card using **scissors**.*

score *verb*
scores, scoring, scored

If you **score** in a game, you get a goal, run, or point.
*He **scored** his second goal of the game.*

scratch *verb*
scratches, scratching, scratched

1 If a sharp thing **scratches** someone or something, it makes small cuts on their skin or on its surface.
*The branches **scratched** my face.*

2 If you **scratch** part of your body, you rub your nails against your skin.
*He **scratched** his head.*

scream *verb*
screams, screaming, screamed

If you **scream**, you shout or cry in a loud, high voice.
*She **screamed** when she saw the spider.*

screen *noun*

screens

A **screen** is a flat surface on which a picture is shown.

*There was dust on the television **screen**.*

sea *noun*

seas

A **sea** is a large area of salt water.

*They swam in the warm **sea**.*

seal *verb*

seals, sealing, sealed

When you **seal** an envelope, you close it by folding part of it and sticking it down.

*He **sealed** the envelope and put on a stamp.*

search *verb*

searches, searching, searched

If you **search** for something or someone, you look for them everywhere.

*I am **searching** for my glasses.*

seaside *noun*

The **seaside** is an area next to the sea.

*I went to spend a few days at the **seaside**.*

season *noun*

seasons

The **seasons** are the four parts of a year: spring, summer, autumn and winter.

*Spring is my favourite **season**.*

seat *noun*

seats

A **seat** is something that you can sit on.

second *adjective*

The **second** thing in a number of things is the one that you count as number two.

*It was the **second** day of his holiday.*

second *noun*

seconds

A **second** is an amount of time. There are sixty **seconds** in one minute.

*For a few **seconds** nobody spoke.*

secret *adjective*

If something is **secret**, only a small number of people know about it, and they do not tell any other people.

*He knew a **secret** place to hide in the garden.*

see *verb*

sees, seeing, saw, seen

1 If you **see** something, you are looking at it or you notice it.
   *The fog was so thick we couldn't **see** anything.*

2 If you **see** someone, you meet them.
   *I **saw** him yesterday.*

seed *noun*

seeds

A **seed** is the small, hard part of a plant from which a new plant grows.

*Plant the **seeds** in the garden.*

seem *verb*

seems, seeming, seemed

If something **seems** to be true, it appears to be true or you think it is true.

*The thunder **seemed** very close.*

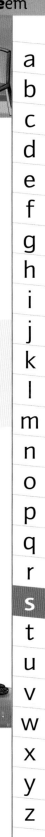

a
b
c
d
e
f
g
h
i
j
k
l
m
n
o
p
q
r
s
t
u
v
w
x
y
z

seen

⇨ Look at **see**.
*She had **seen** the film before.*

sell *verb*
sells, selling, sold

If you **sell** something, you let someone have it in return for money.
*The man **sold** his bike.*

semicircle *noun*
semicircles

A **semicircle** is a half of a circle, or something with this shape.
*The children stood in a **semicircle**.*

send *verb*
sends, sending, sent

When you **send** someone a message or a parcel, you make it go to them.
*I will **send** you a letter when I arrive.*

sensible *adjective*

If you do something **sensible**, you have thought about it a lot first.
*The **sensible** thing is not to touch it.*

sent

⇨ Look at **send**.
*He **sent** a letter home.*

September *noun*

September is the month after August and before October. It has 30 days.

serve *verb*
serves, serving, served

Someone who **serves** customers in a shop or a restaurant helps them with what they want to buy.
*She **served** me coffee and pie.*

set *noun*
sets

A **set** of things is a number of things that belong together.
*I'll need a **set** of clean clothes.*

seven

Seven is the number **7**.

several *adjective*

You use **several** for talking about a number of people or things that is not large but is greater than two.
*There were **several** boxes on the table.*

sew *verb*
sews, sewing, sewed, sewn

When you **sew** pieces of cloth together, you join them using a needle and thread.
*I must **sew** a button on to this shirt.*

sex *noun*
sexes

The **sex** of a person or animal is if it is male or female.
*What **sex** is the baby?*

shadow *noun*
shadows

A **shadow** is a dark shape on a surface that is made when something blocks the light.
*The **shadows** of the trees crossed their path.*

shake *verb*
shakes, shaking, shook, shaken

1 If you **shake** something, you hold it and move it quickly up and down.
  ***Shake** the bottle before you drink.*

2 If someone or something **shakes**, they move quickly backwards and forwards or up and down.
  *My body was **shaking** with cold.*

shallow *adjective*
shallower, shallowest

If something is **shallow**, it is not deep.
*The river is very **shallow** here.*

shape *noun*
shapes

The **shape** of something is the way its outside edges or surfaces look.
*Pasta comes in different **shapes** and sizes.*

share *verb*
shares, sharing, shared

If you **share** something with another person, you both have it or use it.
*We **shared** an ice cream.*

shark *noun*
sharks

A **shark** is a very large fish. **Sharks** have very sharp teeth and some may attack people.

sharp *adjective*
sharper, sharpest

1 A **sharp** point or edge is very thin and can cut through things quickly.
  *Be careful, the scissors are **sharp**.*

2 A **sharp** feeling is sudden and is very big or strong.
  *I felt a **sharp** pain in my right leg.*

shave *verb*
shaves, shaving, shaved

If you **shave**, you remove hair from your face or body by cutting it off.
*Rahim took a bath and **shaved**.*

shed *noun*
sheds

A **shed** is a small building where you store things.
*The house has a large **shed** in the garden.*

she'd

1 **She'd** is short for **she had**.
  ***She'd** already seen them.*

2 **She'd** is also short for **she would**.
  ***She'd** be very happy.*

sheep *noun*
sheep

A **sheep** is a farm animal with thick hair called wool. Farmers keep **sheep** for their wool or for their meat.

sheet *noun*
sheets

1 A **sheet** is a large piece of cloth that you sleep on or cover yourself with in bed.
  *Once a week, we change the **sheets**.*

2 A **sheet** is a piece of paper, glass, plastic, or metal.
  *He folded the **sheets** of paper.*

119

A
B
C
D
E
F
G
H
I
J
K
L
M
N
O
P
Q
R
S
T
U
V
W
X
Y
Z

shelf *noun*
shelves

A **shelf** is a long flat piece of wood on a wall or in a cupboard that you can keep things on.
*Dad took a book from the **shelf**.*

shell *noun*
shells

1 The **shell** of an egg or nut is its hard part.
2 The **shell** of an animal such as a snail is the hard part that covers its back and protects it.

she'll

She'll is short for **she will**.
***She'll** be back.*

she's

She's is short for **she is**.
***She's** a doctor.*

shine *verb*
shines, shining, shone

If something **shines**, it gives out bright light.
*Today it's warm and the sun is **shining**.*

shiny *adjective*
shinier, shiniest

If something is **shiny**, it is bright.
*Her hair was **shiny** and clean.*

ship *noun*
ships

A **ship** is a large boat that carries people or things.
*The **ship** was ready to leave.*

shirt *noun*
shirts

A **shirt** is something you wear on the top part of your body. It has a collar and buttons.

shiver *verb*
shivers, shivering, shivered

If you **shiver**, your body shakes because you are cold or scared.
*She **shivered** with cold.*

shoe *noun*
shoes

Shoes are a type of clothing that you wear on your feet.
*I need a new pair of **shoes**.*

shone

⇨ Look at **shine**.
*The sun **shone** all day.*

shop *noun*
shops

A **shop** is a place that sells things.
*He and his wife run a clothes **shop**.*

shore *noun*
shores

The **shore** of a sea or lake is the land along the edge of it.
*They walked slowly down to the **shore**.*

short *adjective*
shorter, shortest

1 If something is **short**, it does not last very long.
*Last year we all went to the seaside for a **short** holiday.*

2 A **short** thing is small in length, distance, or height.
*She has **short**, straight hair.*

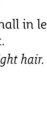

shorts *noun*

Shorts are trousers with short legs.
*He was wearing blue **shorts**.*

should *verb*

You use **should** when you are saying what is the right thing to do.
*He **should** tell us what happened.*

shoulder *noun*
shoulders

Your **shoulders** are the two parts of your body between your neck and the tops of your arms.
*Put your hands on the **shoulders** of the person in front of you.*

shout *verb*
shouts, shouting, shouted

If you **shout**, you say something in a very loud voice.
*He **shouted** something to his brother.*

show *verb*
shows, showing, showed, shown

1 If you **show** someone something, you let them see it.
  *She **showed** me her ring.*

2 If you **show** someone how to do something, you teach them how to do it.
  *She **showed** us how to make pasta.*

shower *noun*
showers

1 A **shower** is a thing that you stand under, that covers you with water so you can wash yourself.
  *I was in the **shower** when the phone rang.*

2 A **shower** is a short period of rain.
  *A few **showers** are expected tomorrow.*

shown

⇨ Look at **show**.
*I've **shown** them how to do it.*

shut *verb*
shuts, shutting, shut

If you **shut** something, you close it.
*Please **shut** the gate.*

shy *adjective*
shyer, shyest

If you are **shy**, you are nervous about talking to people that you do not know well.
*She was a **shy**, quiet girl.*

sick *adjective*
sicker, sickest

If you are **sick**, you are not well.
*He's very **sick** and needs a doctor.*

side *noun*
sides

1 The **side** of something is a place to the left or right of it.
  *On the left **side** of the door there's a door bell.*

2 The **side** of something is also its edge.
  *A square has four **sides**.*

3 The different **sides** in a game are the groups of people who are playing against each other.
  *Both **sides** want to win the match.*

a
b
c
d
e
f
g
h
i
j
k
l
m
n
o
p
q
r
s
t
u
v
w
x
y
z

A B C D E F G H I J K L M N O P Q R S T U V W X Y Z

sign *noun*
signs

1 A **sign** is a mark or a shape that has a special meaning.
*In maths, + is a plus **sign** and - is a minus **sign**.*

2 You can also make a **sign** to somebody by moving something.
*They gave me a **sign** to show that everything was all right.*

silent *adjective*

1 If you are **silent**, you are not talking.
*She was **silent** because she did not know what to say.*

2 If something is **silent**, it is quiet, with no sound at all.
*The room was **silent**.*

silly *adjective*
sillier, silliest

If you are **silly**, you do not behave in a sensible way.
*Don't be **silly**!*

silver *noun*

Silver is a valuable metal.
*He bought her a bracelet made from **silver**.*

sing *verb*
sings, singing, sang, sung

When you **sing**, you make music with your voice.
*I love **singing**.*

sink *noun*
sinks

A **sink** is a large fixed container in a kitchen or a bathroom that you can fill with water.
*The **sink** was filled with dirty dishes.*

sister *noun*
sisters

Your **sister** is a girl or woman who has the same parents as you.
*This is my **sister**.*

sit *verb*
sits, sitting, sat

If you are **sitting** in a chair, your bottom is resting on the chair and the top part of your body is straight.
*Mum was **sitting** in her chair in the kitchen.*

six *noun*

Six is the number **6**.

size *noun*
sizes

The **size** of something is how big or small it is.
*The **size** of the room is about five metres by seven metres.*

skate *noun*
skates

Skates are boots with a thin metal bar on the bottom for moving quickly on ice.

skeleton *noun*
skeletons

A **skeleton** is all the bones in a person's or animal's body.
*A human **skeleton** has more than 200 bones.*

skies
⇨ Look at **sky**.
*The **skies** were grey.*

122

skill *noun*

If you have **skill** you are able to do something well.
*He shows great **skill** on the football field.*

skin *noun*
skins

1 Your **skin** covers your whole body.
   *Too much sun can damage your **skin**.*

2 The **skin** of a fruit or vegetable covers the outside of it.
   *She slipped on a banana **skin**.*

skip *verb*
skips, skipping, skipped

1 If you **skip** along, you move along jumping from one foot to the other.
   *We **skipped** down the street.*

2 If you **skip** something, you decide not to do it.
   *Don't **skip** breakfast.*

skirt *noun*
skirts

A **skirt** is something that women and girls wear. It hangs down from the waist and covers part of the legs.

skull *noun*
skulls

A person's or animal's **skull** is the bones of their head.
*Your **skull** protects your brain.*

sky *noun*
skies

The **sky** is the space around the Earth which you can see when you look up.
*The sun was shining in the **sky**.*

sleep *verb*
sleeps, sleeping, slept

If you **sleep**, you rest with your eyes closed and you do not move.
*Be quiet! The baby is **sleeping**.*

sleeve *noun*
sleeves

The **sleeves** of something you wear are the parts that cover your arms.
*She wore a blue dress with long **sleeves**.*

slept

⇨ Look at **sleep**.
*She **slept** for three hours.*

slice *noun*
slices

A **slice** of something is a thin piece that you cut from a larger piece.
*Would you like a **slice** of bread?*

slide *verb*
slides, sliding, slid

When someone or something **slides**, they move quickly over a surface.
*She **slid** across the ice on her stomach.*

slip *verb*
slips, slipping, slipped

If you **slip**, you slide and fall.
*He **slipped** on the wet grass.*

slipper *noun*
slippers

Slippers are loose, soft shoes that you wear indoors.
*She put on a pair of **slippers**.*

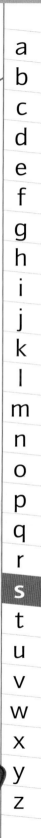

a
b
c
d
e
f
g
h
i
j
k
l
m
n
o
p
q
r
s
t
u
v
w
x
y
z

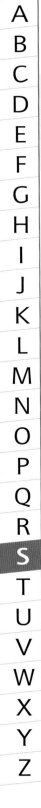

A B C D E F G H I J K L M N O P Q R S T U V W X Y Z

slippery *adjective*

If something is **slippery**, it is smooth or wet, and is difficult to walk on or to hold.
*Be careful—the floor is **slippery**.*

slope *noun*
slopes

A **slope** is the side of a mountain, hill, or valley.
*A steep **slope** leads to the beach.*

slow *adjective*
slower, slowest

If something is **slow**, it does not move quickly.
*The bus was very **slow**.*

slowly

If something moves **slowly**, it does not move quickly.

slug *noun*
slugs

A **slug** is a small animal with a long soft body and no legs that moves very slowly.

small *adjective*
smaller, smallest

If something is **small**, it is not large in size or amount.
*She is **small** for her age.*

smash *verb*
smashes, smashing, smashed

If you **smash** something, it breaks into many pieces.
*The plate **smashed** when it hit the floor.*

smell *noun*
smells

The **smell** of something is what you notice about it when you breathe in through your nose.
*There was a horrible **smell** in the fridge.*

smile *verb*
smiles, smiling, smiled

If you **smile**, the corners of your mouth turn up because you are happy or you think that something is funny.
*He **smiled** at me.*

smoke *noun*

Smoke is the black or white clouds of gas that you see in the air when something burns.
*Thick black **smoke** blew over the city.*

smooth *adjective*
smoother, smoothest

Something **smooth** has no rough parts, lumps, or holes.
*The baby's skin was soft and **smooth**.*

snail *noun*
snails

A **snail** is a small animal with a long, soft body, no legs, and a round shell on its back.

snake *noun*
snakes

A **snake** is a long, thin animal with no legs, that slides along the ground.

sneeze *verb*
sneezes, sneezing, sneezed

When you **sneeze**, you suddenly take in air and then blow it down your nose in a noisy way.
*Cover your nose and mouth when you **sneeze**.*

snow *noun*

Snow is pieces of soft white frozen water that fall from the sky.
*Six inches of **snow** fell last night.*

soap *noun*

Soap is something that you use with water for washing yourself.
*She bought a bar of **soap**.*

sock *noun*
socks

Socks are pieces of cloth that you wear over your foot and ankle, inside your shoes.
*I have a pair of red **socks**.*

sofa *noun*
sofas

A **sofa** is a long, comfortable seat with a back, that two or three people can sit on.

soft *adjective*
softer, softest

1 Something that is **soft** is nice to touch, and not rough or hard.
   *She wiped the baby's face with a **soft** cloth.*
2 A **soft** sound or light is very gentle.
   *There was a **soft** tapping on my door.*

soil *noun*

Soil is the top layer on the surface of the earth in which plants grow.
*The **soil** here is good for growing vegetables.*

sold

⇨ Look at **sell**.
*They **sold** their house today.*

soldier *noun*
soldiers

A **soldier** is someone who is in an army.

solid *adjective*

1 Something that is **solid** stays the same shape if it is in a container or not.
2 Something that is **solid** is not hollow.
   *They had to cut through 5 feet of **solid** rock.*

some

You use **some** to talk about an amount of something.
*Can I have **some** orange juice please?*

somebody

You use **somebody** to talk about a person without saying who you mean.

someone

You use **someone** to talk about a person without saying who you mean.
*I need **someone** to help me.*

something

You use **something** to talk about a thing without saying what it is.
*He knew that there was **something** wrong.*

sometimes

You use **sometimes** to talk about things that do not take place all the time.
***Sometimes** he's a little rude.*

a b c d e f g h i j k l m n o p q r s t u v w x y z

125

somewhere

You use **somewhere** to talk about a place without saying where you mean.
*I've seen him before **somewhere**.*

son *noun*
sons

Someone's **son** is their male child.
*His **son** is seven years old.*

song *noun*
songs

A **song** is words and music sung together.
*She sang a **song**.*

soon *adjective*
sooner, soonest

If you are going to do something **soon** you will do it a very short time from now.
*I'll call you **soon**.*

sore *adjective*
sorer, sorest

If part of your body is **sore**, it is painful.
*I had a **sore** throat.*

sorry *adjective*
sorrier, sorriest

1 If you are **sorry** about something, you feel sad about it.
*I'm **sorry** he's gone.*

2 If you feel **sorry** for someone, you feel sad for them.
*I felt **sorry** for him because nobody listened to him.*

sort *noun*
sorts

The different **sorts** of something are the different types of it.
*What **sort** of school do you go to?*

sound *noun*
sounds

A **sound** is something that you hear.
*He heard the **sound** of a car engine outside.*

soup *noun*

Soup is liquid food made by boiling meat, fish, or vegetables in water.

sour *adjective*

Something that is **sour** has a sharp, nasty taste.
*Lemons have a **sour** taste.*

south *noun*

The **south** is the direction to your right when you are looking towards the place where the sun rises.

space *noun*
spaces

1 You use **space** to talk about an area that is empty.
*They cut down trees to make **space** for houses.*

2 **Space** is the area past the Earth, where the stars and planets are.
*The six astronauts will spend ten days in **space**.*

spade *noun*
spades

A **spade** is a tool that is used for digging.

speak *verb*
speaks, speaking, spoken

When you **speak**, you say words.
*He **spoke** in a whisper.*

special *adjective*

Someone or something that is **special** is better or more important than other people or things.
*Mum made a **special** cake for my birthday.*

speed *noun*
speeds

The **speed** of something is how fast it moves or is done.
*He drove off at high **speed**.*

spell *verb*
spells, spelling, spelled or **spelt**

When you **spell** a word, you write or say each letter in the correct order.
*He **spelled** his name.*

spend *verb*
spends, spending, spent

1   When you **spend** money, you buy things with it.
    *I have **spent** all my money.*
2   To **spend** time or energy is to use it doing something.
    *She **spends** hours working on her garden.*

spider *noun*
spiders

A **spider** is a small animal with eight legs.

spill *verb*
spills, spilling, spilled or **spilt**

If you **spill** a liquid, you make it flow over the edge of a container by accident.
*He always **spilled** the drinks.*

spin *verb*
spins, spinning, spun

If something **spins**, it turns around quickly.
*He made the coin **spin** on his desk.*

spine *noun*
spines

Your **spine** is the row of bones down your back.

splash *verb*
splashes, splashing, splashed

If you **splash** in water, you hit the water in a noisy way.
*The children **splashed** around in the water.*

spoil *verb*
spoils, spoiling, spoiled or **spoilt**

1   If you **spoil** something, you damage it or stop it from working as it should.
    *Don't **spoil** the surprise.*
2   If you **spoil** children, you give them everything they want or ask for.
    *She acted like a **spoilt** child.*

a
b
c
d
e
f
g
h
i
j
k
l
m
n
o
p
q
r
s
t
u
v
w
x
y
z

127

A
B
C
D
E
F
G
H
I
J
K
L
M
N
O
P
Q
R
S
T
U
V
W
X
Y
Z

spoke *noun*
spokes

The **spokes** of a wheel are the bars which join the outside ring to the centre.

spoke

⇨ Look at **speak**.
*She **spoke** in a loud voice.*

spoken

⇨ Look at **speak**.
*He has **spoken** to us.*

spoon *noun*
spoons

A **spoon** is a long tool with a round end that is used for eating, serving or mixing food.
*He stirred his coffee with a **spoon**.*

sport *noun*
sports

Sports are games which need energy and skill.
*She is very good at **sport**.*

spot *noun*
spots

Spots are small, round areas on a surface.
*The leaves are yellow with orange **spots**.*

spot *verb*
spots, spotting, spotted

If you **spot** something or someone, you notice them.
*I didn't **spot** the mistake in his work.*

spout *noun*
spouts

A **spout** is a tube for pouring liquid.
*My kettle has a long **spout**.*

spray *noun*
sprays

Spray is a lot of small drops of water that are thrown into the air.
*The **spray** from the waves covered them.*

spread *verb*
spreads, spreading, spread

1 If you **spread** something somewhere, you open it out.
   *She **spread** a towel on the sand and lay on it.*
2 If you **spread** something on a surface, you put it all over the surface.
   *She was **spreading** butter on the bread.*
3 If something **spreads**, it reaches a larger area.
   *The news **spread** quickly.*

spring *noun*
springs

1 **Spring** is the season between winter and summer when the weather becomes warmer and plants start to grow again.
   *They are getting married next **spring**.*

2 A **spring** is a long piece of metal that goes round and round. It goes back to the same shape after you pull it.
   *The **springs** in the bed were old.*

spun

⇨ Look at **spin**.
*He **spun** the wheel.*

square *noun*
squares

A **square** is a shape with four straight sides that are all the same length.
*Cut the cake in **squares**.*

squirrel *noun*
squirrels

A **squirrel** is a small animal with a long thick tail.
Squirrels live in trees.

stable *noun*
stables

A **stable** is a building where people keep horses.

stairs *noun*

Stairs are steps you walk down or up in a building.
*He walked up the **stairs**.*

stamp *noun*
stamps

A **stamp** is a small piece of paper that you stick on an envelope before you post it.
*She put a **stamp** on the corner of the envelope.*

stamp *verb*
stamps, stamping, stamped

If you **stamp** your foot, you put your foot down very hard on the ground.
*I **stamped** my feet to keep warm.*

stand *verb*
stands, standing, stood

When you are **standing**, you are on your feet.
*She was **standing** beside my bed.*

star *noun*
stars

1 A **star** is a large ball of burning gas in space. **Stars** look like small points of light in the sky.
Stars lit the sky.
2 A **star** is a shape that has four, five, or more points sticking out of it in a pattern.
*How many **stars** are there on the flag?*
3 A **star** is somebody who is famous for doing something, for example acting or singing.
*He's one of the **stars** of a TV show.*

start *verb*
starts, starting, started

1 When something **starts**, it begins.
*When does the film **start**?*
2 If you **start** to do something, you begin to do it.
*She **started** to read her book.*

station *noun*
stations

A **station** is a place where trains or buses stop so that people can get on or off.
*We went to the train **station**.*

stay *verb*
stays, staying, stayed

1 If you **stay** in a place, you do not move away from it.
*She **stayed** in bed until noon.*
2 If you **stay** somewhere, you live there for a short time.
*He **stayed** with them for two weeks.*

steady *adjective*
steadier, steadiest

Something that is **steady** is firm and not shaking.
*He held out a **steady** hand.*

steal *verb*
steals, stealing, stole, stolen

If you **steal** something from someone, you take it without asking or telling them and don't give it back.
*They said he **stole** a bicycle.*

129

A
B
C
D
E
F
G
H
I
J
K
L
M
N
O
P
Q
R
S
T
U
V
W
X
Y
Z

steam *noun*

Steam is the hot gas that water becomes when it boils.
*The **steam** rose into the air.*

steel *noun*

Steel is a very strong metal that is made from iron.
*The door is made of **steel**.*

steep *adjective*
steeper, steepest

A **steep** slope rises quickly and is difficult to go up.
*Some of the hills are very **steep**.*

stem *noun*
stems

The **stem** of a plant is the long, thin part that the flowers and leaves grow on.
*He cut the **stem** and gave her the flower.*

step *noun*
steps

1 If you take a **step**, you lift your foot and put it down in a different place.
*I took a **step** towards him.*

2 A **step** is a flat surface that you put your feet on to walk up or down to somewhere.
*We went down the **steps** into the garden.*

stick *noun*
sticks

A **stick** is a long, thin piece of wood.
*She put some dry **sticks** on the fire.*

stick *verb*
sticks, sticking, stuck

If you **stick** one thing to another, you join them together using glue.
*Now **stick** your picture on a piece of paper.*

stiff *adjective*
stiffer, stiffest

Something that is **stiff** is firm and is not easy to bend.
*The sheet of cardboard was **stiff**.*

still *adjective*
stiller, stillest

If you are **still**, you are not moving.
*Please stand **still**.*

sting *verb*
stings, stinging, stung

If a plant, an animal, or an insect **stings** you, a part of it is pushed into your skin so that you feel a sharp pain.
*She was **stung** by a bee.*

stir *verb*
stirs, stirring, stirred

When you **stir** a liquid, you move it around using a spoon or a stick.

stole

⇨ Look at **steal**.
*They **stole** our car last night.*

stolen

⇨ Look at **steal**.
*All of her money was **stolen**.*

stomach *noun*
stomachs

Your **stomach** is the place inside your body where food goes when you eat it.
*His **stomach** felt full after the meal.*

stone *noun*
stones

1 **Stone** is a hard solid material that is found in the ground. It is often used for building.
*The floor was solid **stone**.*

2 A **stone** is a small piece of rock that is found on the ground.
*He took a **stone** out of his shoe.*

stood

⇨ Look at **stand**.
*He **stood** in the street.*

stop *verb*
stops, stopping, stopped

1 If you **stop** doing something, you do not do it any more.
***Stop** throwing those stones!*

2 If something **stops**, it does not do what it did any more.
*The rain has **stopped**.*

store *verb*
stores, storing, stored

If you **store** something, you keep it somewhere safe.

storm *noun*
storms

A **storm** is very bad weather, with heavy rain and strong winds.
*There will be **storms** along the East Coast.*

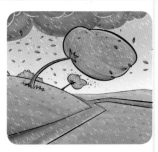

story *noun*
stories

When someone tells you a **story** they describe people and things that are not real, in a way that makes you enjoy hearing about them.
*I'm going to tell you a **story** about four little rabbits.*

straight *adjective*
straighter, straightest

If something is **straight**, it goes one way and does not bend.
*The boat moved in a **straight** line.*

strange *adjective*
stranger, strangest

Something that is **strange** is unusual.
*I had a **strange** dream last night.*

straw *noun*
straws

1 **Straw** is the dry, yellow stems of crops.
*The floor of the barn was covered with **straw**.*

2 A **straw** is a thin tube that you use to suck a drink into your mouth.
*I drank my milk through a **straw**.*

strawberry *noun*
strawberries

A **strawberry** is a small soft red fruit that has a lot of very small seeds on its skin.

stream *noun*
streams

A **stream** is a small narrow river.
*There was a **stream** at the end of the garden.*

a
b
c
d
e
f
g
h
i
j
k
l
m
n
o
p
q
r
s
t
u
v
w
x
y
z

131

A
B
C
D
E
F
G
H
I
J
K
L
M
N
O
P
Q
R
S
T
U
V
W
X
Y
Z

street *noun*
streets

A **street** is a road in a city or a town.
*The **streets** were full of people.*

strength *noun*

Your **strength** is how strong you are.
*Swimming builds up the **strength** of your muscles.*

stretch *verb*
stretches, stretching, stretched

1 Something that **stretches** over an area covers all of it.
*The line of cars **stretched** for miles.*

2 When you **stretch**, you hold out part of your body as far as you can.
*He yawned and **stretched**.*

strict *adjective*
stricter, strictest

A **strict** person expects people to obey rules.
*My parents are very **strict**.*

string *noun*
strings

1 **String** is thin rope that is made of twisted threads.
*He held out a small bag tied with **string**.*

2 The **strings** on an instrument are the thin pieces of wire that are stretched across it and that make sounds when the instrument is played.
*He changed a guitar **string**.*

strip *noun*
strips

A **strip** of something is a long, narrow piece of it.
*Cut a **strip** off a piece of paper, then twist it and stick the two ends together. Then cut it along the middle and see what happens.*

stripe *noun*
stripes

A **stripe** is a long line that is a different colour from the areas next to it.
*She wore a blue skirt with white **stripes**.*

strong *adjective*
stronger, strongest

1 Someone who is **strong** is healthy with good muscles.
*I'm not **strong** enough to carry him.*

2 **Strong** things are not easy to break.
*This **strong** plastic will not crack.*

stuck *adjective*

1 If something is **stuck** in a place, it cannot move.
*His car got **stuck** in the snow.*

2 If you get **stuck**, you can't go on doing something because it is too difficult.
*The teacher will help if you get **stuck**.*

stung

➡ Look at **sting**.
*He was **stung** by a wasp.*

submarine *noun*
submarines

A **submarine** is a ship that can travel under the sea.

subtraction *noun*
Subtraction is when you take one number away from another.

suck *verb*
sucks, sucking, sucked

If you **suck** something, you hold it in your mouth for a long time.
*They **sucked** their sweets.*

sudden *adjective*
Something **sudden** is quick and is not expected.
*The car came to a **sudden** stop.*

suddenly
Suddenly is quickly, without being expected.
Suddenly there was a loud bang.

sugar *noun*
Sugar is a sweet thing that is used for making food and drinks taste sweet.
*Do you take **sugar** in your coffee?*

suit *noun*
suits

A **suit** is a jacket and trousers or a skirt that are made from the same cloth.
*He was wearing a dark **suit**.*

sum *noun*
sums

1 A **sum** of money is an amount of money.
*Large **sums** of money were lost.*

2 In maths, a **sum** is a problem you work out using numbers.
*I have to finish these **sums**.*

summer *noun*
summers

Summer is the season after spring and before autumn. In the **summer** the weather is usually warm or hot.

sun *noun*
suns

The **sun** is the large ball of burning gas in the sky that gives us light.
*The **sun** was now high in the sky.*

Sunday *noun*
Sundays

Sunday is the day after Saturday and before Monday.
*We went for a drive on **Sunday**.*

sunflower *noun*
sunflowers

A **sunflower** is a very tall plant with large yellow flowers.

sung
⇨ Look at **sing**.
*She has **sung** the song many times before.*

sunk
⇨ Look at **sink**.
*The rock has **sunk** to the bottom of the river.*

sunny *adjective*
sunnier, sunniest

When it is **sunny**, the sun is shining.
*The weather was warm and **sunny**.*

a b c d e f g h i j k l m n o p q r s t u v w x y z

133

A B C D E F G H I J K L M N O P Q R S T U V W X Y Z

sunshine *noun*

Sunshine is the light that comes from the sun.
*She was sitting outside in bright **sunshine**.*

supermarket *noun*
supermarkets

A **supermarket** is a large shop that sells all kinds of food and other things for the home.
*Lots of people buy food in a **supermarket**.*

sure *adjective*

If you are **sure** that something is true, you know that it is true.
*I am **sure** my answer is correct.*

surface *noun*
surfaces

The **surface** of something is the flat top part of it or the outside of it.
*There were pen marks on the table's **surface**.*

surname *noun*
surnames

Your **surname** is your last name which you share with other people in your family.

surprise *noun*
surprises

A **surprise** is something that you do not expect.
*I have a **surprise** for you!*

swallow *verb*
swallows, swallowing, swallowed

If you **swallow** something, you make it go from your mouth down into your stomach.
*She took a bite of the apple and **swallowed** it.*

swam

⇨ Look at **swim**.
*She **swam** across the river.*

swan *noun*
swans

A **swan** is a large bird with a long neck, that lives on rivers and lakes.

sweep *verb*
sweeps, sweeping, swept

If you **sweep** an area, you push dirt off it using a brush with a long handle.
*The man in the shop was **sweeping** the floor.*

sweet *adjective*
sweeter, sweetest

Sweet food and drink has a lot of sugar in it.
*Mum gave me a cup of **sweet** tea.*

sweet *noun*
sweets

Sweets are foods that have a lot of sugar.
*Don't eat too many **sweets**.*

swept

⇨ Look at **sweep**.
*The rubbish was **swept** away.*

swim *verb*
swims, swimming, swam, swum

When you **swim**, you move through water by moving your arms and legs.
*She learned to **swim** when she was three.*

swing *verb*
swings, swinging, swung

If something **swings**, it keeps moving backwards and forwards or from side to side through the air.
*She walked beside him with her arms **swinging**.*

switch *noun*
switches

A **switch** is a small button for turning something on or off.
*She pressed the **switch** to turn on the light.*

sword *noun*
swords

A **sword** is like a long knife, with a handle and a long sharp blade.

swum

⇨ Look at **swim**.
*He had never **swum** so far.*

swung

⇨ Look at **swing**.
*She **swung** her bag backwards and forwards.*

Tt

table *noun*
tables

A **table** is a piece of furniture that has legs and a flat top.

tadpole *noun*
tadpoles

A **tadpole** is a small black animal with a round head and a long tail that lives in water. **Tadpoles** grow into frogs or toads.

tail *noun*
tails

An animal's **tail** is the long, thin part at the end of its body.

take *verb*
takes, taking, took, taken

1 If you **take** something, you move it or carry it.
   *She **took** the plates into the kitchen.*

2 If you **take** something that does not belong to you, you steal it.
   *Someone **took** all our money.*

3 If you **take** a vehicle, you ride in it from one place to another.
   *We **took** the bus to school.*

talk *verb*
talks, talking, talked

When you **talk**, you say things to someone.
*She **talked** to him on the phone.*

a
b
c
d
e
f
g
h
i
j
k
l
m
n
o
p
q
r
s
t
u
v
w
x
y
z

A
B
C
D
E
F
G
H
I
J
K
L
M
N
O
P
Q
R
S
T
U
V
W
X
Y
Z

tall *adjective*
taller, tallest

If a person or thing is **tall**, they are higher than usual from top to bottom.

*It was a very **tall** building.*

tame *adjective*
tamer, tamest

If an animal or bird is **tame**, it is not afraid of people and will not try to hurt them.

tap *verb*
taps, tapping, tapped

If you **tap** something, you hit it but you do not use a lot of strength.

*He **tapped** on the door and went in.*

tape *noun*

Tape is a long, thin strip of plastic that has glue on one side. You use **tape** to stick things together.

*He wrapped the parcel with paper and **tape**.*

taste *verb*
tastes, tasting, tasted

If you **taste** something, you eat or drink a small amount of it to see what it is like.

*She **tasted** the soup and then added some salt.*

taught

⇨ Look at **teach**.
*My mum **taught** me to read.*

tea *noun*

1 **Tea** is a drink. You make it by pouring hot water on to the dry leaves of a plant called the **tea** bush.

2 **Tea** is also a meal that you eat in the afternoon or the early evening.

teach *verb*
teaches, teaching, taught

If you **teach** someone something, you help them to understand it or you show them how to do it.

*He **teaches** people how to play the piano.*

teacher *noun*
teachers

A **teacher** is a person whose job is to teach other people. **Teachers** usually work in schools.

team *noun*
teams

A **team** is a group of people who work together, or who play a sport together against another group.

*He is in the school football **team**.*

tear *noun*
tears

Tears are the liquid that comes out of your eyes when you cry.

*Her face was wet with **tears**.*

tear *verb*
tears, tearing, tore, torn

If you **tear** something, you pull it into pieces or make a hole in it.

*Try not to **tear** the paper.*

teeth

⇨ Look at **tooth**.

*Clean your **teeth** before you go to bed.*

telephone *noun*
telephones

A **telephone** is a machine that you use to talk to someone who is in another place.

television *noun*
televisions

A **television** is a machine that shows moving pictures with sound on a screen.

tell *verb*
tells, telling, told

1 If you **tell** someone something, you let them know about it.
  ***Tell** me about your holiday.*

2 If you **tell** someone to do something, you say that they must do it.
  *She **told** me to go away.*

3 If you can **tell** something, you know it.
  *I can **tell** that he is angry.*

ten *noun*

Ten is the number .

tent *noun*
tents

A **tent** is made of strong material that is held up with long pieces of metal and ropes. You sleep in a **tent** when you stay in a camp.

term *noun*
terms

A **term** is one of the parts of a school year. There are usually three **terms** in a year.

terrible *adjective*

If something is **terrible**, it is very bad.
*That was a **terrible** film.*

test *verb*
tests, testing, tested

If you **test** something, you try it to see what it is like, or how it works.
***Test** the water to see if it is warm.*

test *noun*
tests

A **test** is something you do to show how much you know or what you can do.
*The teacher gave us a maths **test**.*

thank *verb*
thanks, thanking, thanked

When you **thank** someone, you tell them that you are pleased about something they have given you or have done for you. You usually do this by saying "Thank you".
*I **thanked** him for my present.*

theatre *noun*
theatres

A **theatre** is a building where you go to see people acting stories, singing, or dancing.

a
b
c
d
e
f
g
h
i
j
k
l
m
n
o
p
q
r
s
t
u
v
w
x
y
z

their

You use **their** to say that something belongs to a group of people, animals, or things.
*They took off **their** coats.*

theirs

You use **theirs** to say that something belongs to a group of people, animals, or things.
*The house next to **theirs** was empty.*

then

1 **Then** means at that time.
   *He wasn't as rich **then** as he is now.*
2 You also use **then** to say that one thing happens after another.
   *She said good night, **then** went to bed.*

there

1 You use **there** to say that something is in a place or is happening, or to make someone notice it.
   ***There** are flowers on the table.*
2 **There** also means to a place, or at a place.
   *I have never been **there** before.*

there's

There's is short for **there is**.
***There's** nothing in the box.*

they

You use **they** when you are talking about more than one person, animal, or thing.
***They** are all in the same class.*

they'd

1 **They'd** is short for **they had**.
2 **They'd** is also short for **they would**.
   *The boys said **they'd** come back later.*

they'll

They'll is short for **they will**.
***They'll** be here on Monday.*

they're

They're is short for **they are**.
***They're** going to the circus.*

they've

They've is short for **they have**.
***They've** gone away.*

thick *adjective*
thicker, thickest

1 If something is **thick**, it is deep or wide between one side and the other.
   *He cut a **thick** slice of bread.*
2 If a liquid is **thick**, it flows slowly.
   *This soup is very **thick**.*

thigh *noun*
thighs

Your **thighs** are the parts of your legs that are above your knees.
*His **thighs** ached from climbing the hill.*

thin *adjective*
thinner, thinnest

1 If something is **thin**, it is narrow between one side and the other.
   *The book is printed on very **thin** paper.*
2 If a person or animal is **thin**, they are not fat and they do not weigh much.
   *He was a tall, **thin** man.*

thing *noun*
things

A **thing** is something that is not a plant, an animal, or a human being.
*What's that **thing** lying in the road?*

think *verb*
thinks, thinking, thought

1 If you **think** something, you believe that it is true.
*I **think** it's a great idea.*

2 When you **think**, you use your mind.
*I tried to **think** what to do.*

thirsty *adjective*
thirstier, thirstiest

If you are **thirsty**, you want to drink something.

thought
⇨ Look at **think**.
*I **thought** they were here.*

thread *noun*
threads

Thread is a long, thin piece of cotton or wool that you use to sew cloth.

three *noun*
Three is the number **3**.

threw
⇨ Look at **throw**.
*She **threw** her coat on to a chair.*

throat *noun*
throats

1 Your **throat** is the back part of your mouth that you use to swallow and to breathe.

2 Your **throat** is also the front part of your neck.

through
Through means going all the way from one side of something to the other side.
*We walked **through** the forest.*

throw *verb*
throws, throwing, threw, thrown

When you **throw** something you are holding, you move your hand quickly and let the thing go, so that it moves through the air.
***Throw** the ball to me.*

thumb *noun*
thumbs

Your **thumb** is the short, thick finger on the side of your hand.
*The baby sucked its **thumb**.*

thunder *noun*
Thunder is the loud noise that you sometimes hear from the sky when there is a storm.

Thursday *noun*
Thursdays

Thursday is the day after Wednesday and before Friday.
*I saw her on **Thursday**.*

a b c d e f g h i j k l m n o p q r s t u v w x y z

139

A
B
C
D
E
F
G
H
I
J
K
L
M
N
O
P
Q
R
S
T
U
V
W
X
Y
Z

tidy *adjective*
tidier, tidiest

Something that is **tidy** is neat, with everything in its proper place.

tie *verb*
ties, tying, tied

If you **tie** something, you fasten it with string or a rope.
*He **tied** the dog to the fence.*

tie *noun*
ties

A **tie** is a long, narrow piece of cloth that you tie a knot in and wear around your neck with a shirt.

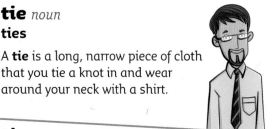

tiger *noun*
tigers

A **tiger** is a large wild cat that has orange fur with black stripes.

tight *adjective*
tighter, tightest

1 If clothes are **tight**, they are so small that they fit very close to your body.
*His trousers were very **tight**.*

2 Something that is **tight** is fastened so that it is not easy to move it.
*The string was tied in a **tight** knot.*

time *noun*

1 **Time** is how long something takes to happen.
We measure **time** in minutes, hours, days, weeks, months, and years.
*I've known him for a long **time**.*

2 The **time** is a moment in the day that you describe in hours and minutes.
*"What **time** is it?"—"Ten past five."*

tin *noun*
tins

1 **Tin** is a kind of soft, pale grey metal.

2 A **tin** is a metal container for food.
*She opened a **tin** of beans.*

tiny *adjective*
tinier, tiniest

If something is **tiny**, it is very small.
*Our new kitten is **tiny**.*

tired *adjective*

If you are **tired**, you need to rest or get some sleep.

toad *noun*
toads

A **toad** is a small animal that looks like a frog.
Toads have rough, dry skin and live on land.

today

Today means the day that is happening now.
*I feel much better **today**.*

toe *noun*
toes

Your **toes** are the five parts at the end of each foot.
*I'm sorry I stood on your **toes**.*

together

If people do something **together**, they do it with each other.
*We played football **together**.*

140

told

⇨ Look at **tell**.
*We **told** them the answer.*

tomato *noun*
tomatoes

A **tomato** is a soft red fruit with a lot of juice.

tomorrow

Tomorrow is the day after today.
*I'll see you **tomorrow**.*

tongue *noun*
tongues

Your **tongue** is the soft part inside your mouth that moves when you eat or talk.

tonight

Tonight is the evening or night that will come at the end of today.
*We're going out **tonight**.*

too

1 **Too** means also.
*Can I come **too**?*

2 You also use **too** to mean more than you want or need.
*The TV is **too** loud.*

took

⇨ Look at **take**.
*It **took** me hours.*

tool *noun*
tools

A **tool** is something that you hold in your hands and use to do a job.

tooth *noun*
teeth

1 Your **teeth** are the hard, white things in your mouth that you use to bite and chew food.
*I clean my **teeth** twice a day.*

2 The **teeth** of a comb, a saw, or a zip are the parts that are in a row along its edge.

top *noun*
tops

1 The **top** of something is the highest part of it.
*We climbed to the **top** of the hill.*

2 The **top** of something is also the part that fits over the end of it.
*He took the **top** off the jar.*

tore

⇨ Look at **tear**.
*She **tore** her dress on a nail.*

torn

⇨ Look at **tear**.
*He has **torn** the cover of the book.*

tortoise *noun*
tortoises

A **tortoise** is an animal with a hard shell on its back. It can pull its head and legs inside the shell. **Tortoises** move very slowly.

touch *verb*
touches, touching, touched

1 If you **touch** something, you put your fingers or your hand on it.
*The baby **touched** my face.*

2 If one thing **touches** another, they are so close that there is no space between them.
*Her feet **touched** the floor.*

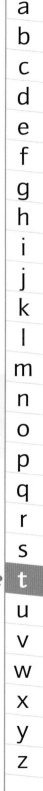

a
b
c
d
e
f
g
h
i
j
k
l
m
n
o
p
q
r
s
t
u
v
w
x
y
z

141

A
B
C
D
E
F
G
H
I
J
K
L
M
N
O
P
Q
R
S
T
U
V
W
X
Y
Z

towards

Towards means in the direction of something.
*He moved **towards** the door.*

towel *noun*
towels

A **towel** is a piece of thick, soft cloth that you use to get yourself dry.

town *noun*
towns

A **town** is a place with a lot of streets, buildings, and shops, where people live and work.

toy *noun*
toys

A **toy** is something that you play with.

tractor *noun*
tractors

A **tractor** is a vehicle with big wheels at the back. **Tractors** are used on a farm to pull machines and other heavy things.

traffic *noun*

Traffic is all the vehicles that are on a road at the same time.
*There is a lot of **traffic** in the town today.*

train *noun*
trains

A **train** is a long vehicle that is pulled by an engine along a railway line.

travel *verb*
travels, travelling, travelled

When you **travel**, you go from one place to another.
*He **travelled** to many different countries.*

tree *noun*
trees

A **tree** is a very tall plant with branches, leaves, and a hard main part that is called a trunk.

triangle *noun*
triangles

1   A **triangle** is a shape with three straight sides.

2   A **triangle** is also an instrument made of metal in the shape of a **triangle** that you hit with a stick to make music.

trick *verb*
tricks, tricking, tricked

If someone **tricks** you, they make you believe something that is not true so that you will do what they want.
*They **tricked** her into giving them money.*

tried

⇨ Look at **try**.
*They **tried** their best.*

tries

⇨ Look at **try**.
*She **tries** to help.*

trip *noun*
trips

When you go on a **trip**, you travel to a place and then come back.
*We went on a **trip** to the park.*

trousers *noun*

Trousers are things that you can wear. They cover the part of your body below the waist, and each leg.
*He was wearing brown **trousers**.*

truck *noun*
trucks

A **truck** is a large vehicle that is used to carry things.

true *adjective*

1 If a story is **true**, it really happened.
*Everything she said was **true**.*

2 If something is **true**, it is right or correct.
*Is it **true** that you have six cats?*

trunk *noun*
trunks

1 A **trunk** is the thick stem of a tree. The branches and roots grow from the **trunk**.

2 An elephant's **trunk** is its long nose. Elephants use their **trunks** to suck up water and to lift things.

3 A **trunk** is also a large, strong box that you use to keep things in.

try *verb*
tries, trying, tried

1 If you **try** to do something, you do it as well as you can.
*I will **try** to come tomorrow.*

2 If you **try** something, you test it to see what it is like or how it works.
*Would you like to **try** my new bike?*

tube *noun*
tubes

1 A **tube** is a long, round, hollow piece of metal, rubber, or plastic.
*The liquid goes through the **tube** into the bottle.*

2 A **tube** is also a soft metal or plastic container that you press to make what is in it come out.
*He bought a **tube** of glue.*

Tuesday *noun*
Tuesdays

Tuesday is the day after Monday and before Wednesday.
*He came home on **Tuesday**.*

tune *noun*
tunes

A **tune** is a piece of music that is nice to listen to.
*She played a **tune** on the piano.*

tunnel *noun*
tunnels

A **tunnel** is a long hole that goes below the ground or through a hill.

143

A
B
C
D
E
F
G
H
I
J
K
L
M
N
O
P
Q
R
S
T
U
V
W
X
Y
Z

turn *verb*
turns, turning, turned

1 When you **turn**, you move in a different direction.
   *He **turned** and walked away.*
2 When something **turns**, it moves around in a circle.
   *The wheels **turned** slowly.*
3 If one thing **turns** into another thing, it becomes that thing.
   *The tadpole **turned** into a frog.*
4 When you **turn** a machine on, you make it start working. When you **turn** it off, you make it stop working.
   *I **turned** off the television.*

tusk *noun*
tusks

An elephant's **tusks** are the two very long, curved teeth that it has beside its trunk.

TV *noun*
TVs

TV is short for **television**.
*What's on **TV**?*

twelve *noun*

Twelve is the number **12**.

twice

If something happens **twice**, it happens two times.
*I've met him **twice**.*

twig *noun*
twigs

A **twig** is a very small, thin branch that grows on a tree or a bush.

twin *noun*
twins

If two people are **twins**, they have the same parents and they were born on the same day. **Twins** often look alike.

twist *verb*
twists, twisting, twisted

If you **twist** something, you turn one end of it in one direction while you hold the other end or turn it in the opposite direction.
*She **twisted** the towel in her hands.*

two *noun*

Two is the number .

tying

⇨ Look at **tie**.
*He was **tying** the two pieces of rope together.*

type *noun*
types

A **type** of something is the kind of thing that it is.
*Owls are a **type** of bird.*

type *verb*
types, typing, typed

If you **type** something, you write it with a machine, for example a computer.
*She **typed** a letter.*

tyre *noun*
tyres

A **tyre** is a thick circle made of strong rubber that goes round a wheel. **Tyres** usually have air inside them.

Uu

ugly *adjective*
uglier, ugliest

If something is **ugly**, it is not nice to look at.
*The monster had an **ugly** face.*

umbrella *noun*
umbrellas

An **umbrella** is a long stick that is joined to a cover made of cloth or plastic. You hold an **umbrella** over your head so that you will not get wet in the rain.

uncle *noun*
uncles

Your **uncle** is the brother of your mother or father, or the husband of your aunt.

understand *verb*
understands, understanding, understood

If you **understand** something, you know what it means or why or how it happens.
*I didn't **understand** what he said.*

underwear *noun*

Your **underwear** is the name for the clothes that you wear next to your skin, under all your other clothes.

undress *verb*
undresses, undressing, undressed

When you **undress**, you take off your clothes.

uniform *noun*
uniforms

A **uniform** is a special set of clothes that some people wear to show what job they do, or some children wear to show what school they go to.
*I put on my school **uniform**.*

until

If something happens **until** a time, it happens before that time and then stops at that time.
*Wait here **until** I come back.*

unusual *adjective*

If something is **unusual**, it does not happen very often.
*It is **unusual** for him to be late.*

up

When something moves **up**, it moves from a lower place to a higher place.
*She ran **up** the stairs.*

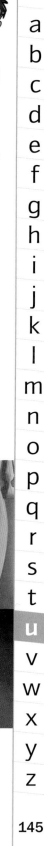

upon

Upon means the same as **on**.
*He stood **upon** the bridge.*

A
B
C
D
E
F
G
H
I
J
K
L
M
N
O
P
Q
R
S
T
U
V
W
X
Y
Z

upset *adjective*

If you are **upset**, you are sad because something bad has happened.
*I was **upset** when my brother broke my doll.*

upside down

1 If something is **upside down**, the part that is usually at the bottom is at the top.
*The picture was **upside down**.*

2 If you hang **upside down**, your head is below your feet.

urgent *adjective*

If something is **urgent**, it is very important and you need to do something about it quickly.
*This problem is **urgent**.*

use *verb*
uses, using, used

If you **use** something, you do something with it.
***Use** a cloth to clean the table.*

useful *adjective*

If something is **useful**, you can use it to do something or to help you in some way.

usual *adjective*

Something that is **usual** is what happens most often.
*He arrived at his **usual** time.*

usually

If something **usually** happens, it is the thing that happens most often.
*I **usually** take the bus to school.*

Vv

valley *noun*
valleys

A **valley** is a low area of land between hills.

valuable *adjective*

If something is **valuable**, it is worth a lot of money.

van *noun*
vans

A **van** is a covered vehicle larger than a car but smaller than a lorry. People use **vans** for carrying things.

vase *noun*
vases

A **vase** is a jar for flowers.

vegetable *noun*
vegetables

Vegetables are plants that you can cook and eat.

vehicle *noun*
vehicles

A **vehicle** is a machine that carries people or things from one place to another.

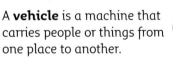

verb *noun*
verbs

A **verb** is a word like 'sing,' 'feel,' or 'eat' that you use for saying what someone or something does.

very

Very is used before a word to make it stronger.

*She had a **very** bad dream.*

vet *noun*
vets

A **vet** is a doctor for animals.

video *noun*
videos

A **video** is a copy of a film or television programme.

village *noun*
villages

A **village** is a small town.

voice *noun*
voices

Your **voice** is the sound that comes from your mouth when you talk or sing.

volcano *noun*
volcanoes

A **volcano** is a mountain that throws out hot, liquid rock and fire.

vote *verb*
votes, voting, voted

When a group of people **vote**, everybody shows what they want to do, usually by writing on a piece of paper or by putting their hands up.

*We **voted** to send money to people who were in the earthquake.*

waist *noun*
waists

Your **waist** is the middle part of your body.

waist

wait *verb*
waits, waiting, waited

When you **wait** for something or someone, you spend time doing very little, before something happens.

wake *verb*
wakes, waking, woke, woken

When you **wake** up, you stop sleeping.

walk *verb*
walks, walking, walked

When you **walk**, you move along by putting one foot in front of the other.

wall *noun*
walls

A **wall** is one of the sides of a building or a room.

want *verb*
wants, wanting, wanted

If you **want** something, you would like to have it.

a
b
c
d
e
f
g
h
i
j
k
l
m
n
o
p
q
r
s
t
u
v
w
x
y
z

147

A B C D E F G H I J K L M N O P Q R S T U V W X Y Z

war *noun*

wars

A **war** is when countries or groups fight each other.

wardrobe *noun*

wardrobes

A **wardrobe** is a tall cupboard that you can hang your clothes in.

warm *adjective*

warmer, warmest

Something that is **warm** is not cold, but not hot.
*The bread is still **warm** from the oven.*

warn *verb*

warns, warning, warned

If you **warn** someone about a possible problem or danger, you tell them about it.
*I **warned** them not to go.*

was

⇨ Look at **be**.
*It **was** my birthday yesterday.*

wash *verb*

washes, washing, washed

If you **wash** something, you clean it using soap and water.

wasn't

Wasn't is short for **was not**.
*She **wasn't** happy.*

wasp *noun*

wasps

A **wasp** is an insect with wings and yellow and black stripes across its body. **Wasps** can sting people.

waste *verb*

wastes, wasting, wasted

If you **waste** time, money, or energy, you use too much of it on something that is not important.
*It's important not to **waste** water.*

watch *verb*

watches, watching, watched

If you **watch** something, you look at it for a period of time.

watch *noun*

watches

A **watch** is a small clock that you wear on your wrist.

water *noun*

Water is a clear liquid that has no colour, taste or smell. It falls from clouds as rain.

wave *noun*

waves

Waves on the surface of the sea are the parts that move up and down.
*The **waves** broke over the rocks.*

wave *verb*

waves, waving, waved

If you **wave** your hand, you move it from side to side, usually to say hello or goodbye.

wax *noun*

Wax is a soft material that melts when you make it hot. It is used to make crayons and candles.

way *noun*

ways

1 A **way** of doing something is how you do it.
*This is the **way** to throw the ball.*
2 The **way** to a place is how you get there.
*We're going the wrong **way**!*

weak *adjective*

weaker, weakest

If someone or something is **weak**, they are not strong.
*When she spoke, her voice was **weak**.*

wear *verb*

wears, wearing, wore, worn

When you **wear** clothes, shoes or glasses, you have them on your body.
*What are you going to **wear** today?*

weather *noun*

The **weather** is what it is like outside, for example if it is raining or sunny.
*What will the **weather** be like tomorrow?*

web *noun*

webs

1 The **Web** is made up of a very large number of websites all joined together. You can use it anywhere in the world to search for information.
2 A **web** is the thin net made by a spider from a string that comes out of its body.

website *noun*

websites

A **website** is a place on the Internet that gives you information.
*Our school has a **website**.*

we'd

1 **We'd** is short for **we had**.
We'd left early in the morning.
2 **We'd** is also short for **we would**.
We'd like you to come with us.

wedding *noun*

weddings

A **wedding** is when two people get married.

Wednesday *noun*

Wednesdays

Wednesday is the day after Tuesday and before Thursday.

week *noun*

weeks

A **week** is a period of seven days.
*This is the last **week** of the holidays.*

weekend *noun*

weekends

The **weekend** is the days at the end of the week, when you do not go to school or work.

weigh *verb*

weighs, weighing, weighed

If you **weigh** something or someone, you measure how heavy they are.
*I **weigh** more than my brother.*

a
b
c
d
e
f
g
h
i
j
k
l
m
n
o
p
q
r
s
t
u
v
w
x
y
z

weight *noun*

The **weight** of a person or thing is how heavy they are.
*What is your **weight** and height?*

well
better, best

If you do something **well**, you do it in a good way.
*He draws **well**.*

well *noun*

A **well** is a deep hole in the ground from which people take water, oil or gas.

we'll

We'll is short for **we will**.
***We'll** come along later.*

went

⇨ Look at **go**.
*They **went** to school.*

were

⇨ Look at **be**.
*They **were** at home yesterday.*

we're

We're is short for **we are**.
***We're** late!*

weren't

Weren't is short for **were not**.
*They **weren't** at school yesterday.*

west *noun*

The **west** is the direction ahead of you when you are looking towards the place where the sun goes down.

wet *adjective*
wetter, wettest

If something is **wet**, it is covered in water.

we've

We've is short for **we have**.
***We've** got lots of books.*

whale *noun*
whales

Whales are very large sea mammals.
***Whales** breathe through a hole on the top of their heads.*

what

You use **what** in questions when you ask for information.
***What** time is it?*

wheat *noun*

Wheat is a crop. People make flour and bread from **wheat**.

wheel *noun*
wheels

Wheels are round and they turn.
Bikes and cars move along on **wheels**.

wheelchair *noun*
wheelchairs

A **wheelchair** is a chair with wheels that you use if you cannot walk.

when

You use **when** to ask what time something happened or will happen.
***When** are you leaving?*

A B C D E F G H I J K L M N O P Q R S T U V W X Y Z

where

You use **where** to ask questions about the place something is in.
Where's your house?

which

You use **which** when you want help to choose between things.
Which shoes should I put on?

while

If one thing happens **while** another thing is happening, the two things are happening at the same time.
*She goes to work **while** her children are at school.*

whisper *verb*
whispers, whispering, whispered

When you **whisper**, you speak in a very quiet voice.
*Don't you know it's rude to **whisper**?*

whistle *verb*
whistles, whistling, whistled

When you **whistle**, you make sounds like music by blowing hard.

white *noun/adjective*

White is the colour of snow or milk.
*His shirt is **white**.*

who

You use **who** in questions when you ask about someone's name.
Who won the quiz?

who'd

Who'd is short for **who would**.
Who'd like to come with me?

whole *adjective*

The **whole** of something is all of it.
*Have the **whole** cake.*

who'll

Who'll is short for **who will**.
Who'll go and find her?

whose

You use **whose** to ask who something belongs to.
Whose bag is this?

why

You use **why** when you are asking about the reason for something.
Why did you do it?

wide *adjective*
wider, widest

Something that is **wide** is a large distance from one side to the other.
*The bed is too **wide** for this room.*

width *noun*

The **width** of something is the distance from one side to another.
*Measure the full **width** of the table.*

wife *noun*
wives

A man's **wife** is the woman he is married to.

A
B
C
D
E
F
G
H
I
J
K
L
M
N
O
P
Q
R
S
T
U
V
W
X
Y
Z

wild *adjective*
wilder, wildest

Wild animals or plants live or grow in nature, and people do not take care of them.

will *verb*

You use **will** to talk about things that are going to happen in the future.
*Mum **will** be angry.*

win *verb*
wins, winning, won

If you **win**, you do better than everyone.
*You've **won** first prize!*

wind *noun*
Wind is air that moves.

wind *verb*
winds, winding, wound

1 If a road or river **winds**, it twists and turns.

2 When you **wind** something long around something, you wrap it around several times.
*She **wound** the rope around her waist.*

window *noun*
windows

A **window** is a space in the wall of a building or in the side of a vehicle that has glass in it.

wing *noun*
wings

The **wings** of birds, insects or aeroplanes are the parts that keep them in the air.

winner *noun*
winners

The **winner** of a race or competition is the person who wins it.
*Our teacher will give the prizes to the **winners**.*

winter *noun*
winters

Winter is the season after autumn and before spring. In the **winter** the weather is usually cold.

wipe *verb*
wipes, wiping, wiped

If you **wipe** dirt or liquid from something, you remove it using a cloth or your hands.
*She **wiped** the tears from her eyes.*

wire *noun*
wires

A **wire** is a long thin piece of metal.
*The birds were sitting on a telephone **wire**.*

wise *adjective*
wiser, wisest

A **wise** person can decide on the right thing to do.

wish *verb*
wishes, wishing, wished

If you **wish** something, you would like it to be true.
*I **wish** I had a pet.*

witch *noun*
witches

In children's stories, a **witch** is a woman who has magic powers that she uses to do bad things.

with

1 If one person is **with** another, they are together in one place.
*He's watching a film **with** his friends.*

2 You use **with** to say that someone has something.
*My daughter is the girl **with** brown hair.*

without

If you do something **without** someone, they are not in the same place as you are, or they are not doing the same thing as you.
*He went **without** me.*

wives

⇨ Look at **wife**.
*The men bought flowers for their **wives**.*

wizard *noun*
wizards

In children's stories, a **wizard** is a man who has magic powers.

woke

⇨ Look at **wake**.
*They **woke** early.*

woken

⇨ Look at **wake**.
*We were **woken** by a loud noise.*

wolf *noun*
wolves

A **wolf** is a wild animal that looks like a large dog.

woman *noun*
women

A **woman** is an adult female person.

won

⇨ Look at **win**.
*She **won** first prize.*

won't

Won't is short for **will not**.
*I **won't** be late.*

wood *noun*
woods

1 **Wood** is the hard material that trees are made of.

2 A **wood** is a large area of trees growing near each other.

wool *noun*

Wool is a material made from the fur of sheep. It is used for making things such as clothes.

word *noun*
words

Words are things that you say or write.
*Some **words** are short and some are long.*

wore

⇨ Look at **wear**.
*She **wore** a red dress.*

work *verb*
works, working, worked

1 When you **work**, you do something that uses a lot of your time or effort.
*We **work** hard all day.*

2 If a machine **works**, it does its job.
*The TV isn't **working**.*

a b c d e f g h i j k l m n o p q r s t u v **w** x y z

153

A
B
C
D
E
F
G
H
I
J
K
L
M
N
O
P
Q
R
S
T
U
V
W
X
Y
Z

world *noun*
worlds

The **world** is the earth, the planet we live on.

worm *noun*
worms

A **worm** is a small animal with a long thin body, no bones, and no legs.

worn

⇨ Look at **wear**.
*Have you **worn** this?*

worry *verb*
worries, worrying, worried

If you **worry**, you keep thinking about problems that you have or about nasty things that might happen.

worse

If something is **worse** than another thing, it is not as good.
*My spelling is **worse** than yours.*

worst

If something is the **worst**, all other things are better.
*That was the **worst** day in my life.*

worth

If something is **worth** a sum of money, that's how much you could sell it for.
*This gold ring is **worth** a lot of money.*

would *verb*

You use **would** to say that someone agreed to do something. You use **would not** to say that they refused to do something.
*They said they **would** come to my party.*

wound

⇨ Look at **wind**.
*She **wound** the rope around her wrist.*

wrap *verb*
wraps, wrapping, wrapped

When you **wrap** something, you fold paper or cloth around it to cover it.
*I didn't have enough paper to **wrap** the present.*

wrist *noun*
wrists

Your **wrist** is the part of your body between your arm and your hand. Your **wrists** bend when you move your hands.

write *verb*
writes, writing, wrote, written

When you **write** something, you use a pen or pencil to make letters, words, or numbers.
*He **wrote** his name in the book.*

writing *noun*

Writing is words that have been written or printed.
*Can you read my **writing**?*

written

⇨ Look at **write**.
*My uncle has **written** a song.*

wrong *adjective*

1 If you say that an answer is **wrong**, you mean that it is not right.
   *No, you've got that **wrong**!*

2 If you say that something someone does is **wrong**, you mean that it is bad.
   *It is **wrong** to hurt animals.*

Xx

X-ray *noun*
X-rays

An **X-ray** is a picture of the inside of someone's body.
The X-ray showed that my arm was broken.

xylophone *noun*
xylophones

A **xylophone** is an instrument made of flat pieces of wood or metal in a row. You hit the pieces with a stick to make different sounds.

Yy

yacht *noun*
yachts

A **yacht** is a large boat with sails or an engine, used for races or for making trips.

yawn *verb*
yawns, yawning, yawned

If you **yawn**, you open your mouth very wide and breathe in more air than usual because you are tired or bored.

year *noun*
years

A **year** is a period of twelve months, beginning on January 1 and finishing on December 31.

yell *verb*
yells, yelling, yelled

If you **yell**, you shout something, often because you are angry.
She yelled at him to stop.

yellow *noun/adjective*

Yellow is the colour of lemons or butter.
Her favourite colour is yellow.

yes

You say **yes** to agree with someone or to say that something is true, or if you want something.

yesterday

Yesterday is the day before today.
There was no school yesterday.

yogurt or **yoghurt** *noun*
yogurts or **yoghurts**

Yogurt is a thick liquid food that is made from milk.
I like strawberry yogurt more than peach yogurt.

yolk *noun*
yolks

The **yolk** of an egg is the yellow part.

you

You means the person or people that someone is talking or writing to.
Can I help you?

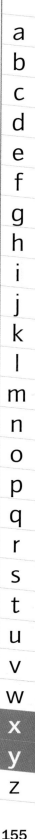

a b c d e f g h i j k l m n o p q r s t u v w x y z

A B C D E F G H I J K L M N O P Q R S T U V W X Y Z

you'd

1 **You'd** is short for **you had**.
I thought you'd told him.

2 **You'd** is also short for **you would**.
You'd like it a lot.

you'll

You'll is short for **you will**.
You'll be late!

young *adjective*
younger, youngest

A **young** person, animal, or plant has not lived for very long.
A kitten is a young cat.

your

You use **your** to show that something belongs to the people that you are talking to.
I do like your name.

you're

You're is short for **you are**.
You're very early!

yours

Yours refers to something belonging to the people that you are talking to.
His hair is longer than yours.

yourself
yourselves

Yourself means you alone.
You'll hurt yourself.

you've

You've is short for **you have**.
You've got very long legs.

zebra *noun*
zebras

A **zebra** is a wild African animal like a horse with black and white stripes.

zero *noun*
zeros or **zeroes**

Zero is the number **0**.

zip *noun*
zips

A **zip** is two long rows of little teeth and a piece that slides along them. You pull this to open or close the **zip**.

zoo *noun*
zoos

A **zoo** is a place where live animals are kept so that people can look at them.